FORWARD MOTION

*On the Road
In Scooters and Wheelchairs*

stories edited by

RUTH OTTAWAY SHERER

Trafford
PUBLISHING

Order this book online at www.trafford.com/06-3257
or email orders@trafford.com

Most Trafford titles are also available at major online book retailers.

Note for Librarians: A cataloguing record for this book is available from Library
and Archives Canada at www.collectionscanada.ca/amicus/index-e.html

Printed in Victoria, BC, Canada.

ISBN: 978-1-4251-1498-5

*We at Trafford believe that it is the responsibility of us all, as both individuals
and corporations, to make choices that are environmentally and socially sound.
You, in turn, are supporting this responsible conduct each time you purchase a
Trafford book, or make use of our publishing services. To find out how you are
helping, please visit www.trafford.com/responsiblepublishing.html*

*Our mission is to efficiently provide the world's finest, most comprehensive
book publishing service, enabling every author to experience success.
To find out how to publish your book, your way, and have it available
worldwide, visit us online at www.trafford.com/10510*

 www.trafford.com

North America & international
toll-free: 1 888 232 4444 (USA & Canada)
phone: 250 383 6864 ♦ fax: 250 383 6804 ♦ email: info@trafford.com

The United Kingdom & Europe
phone: +44 (0)1865 722 113 ♦ local rate: 0845 230 9601
facsimile: +44 (0)1865 722 868 ♦ email: info.uk@trafford.com

10 9 8 7 6 5 4

This book is dedicated
with love and joy
to the memory of
Donald R. McNeil
July 5, 1923—March 8, 1996

and in honor of my brother
James H. Ottaway Jr.
whose loving carrot-and-stick persistence
finally succeeded
in my getting this manuscript
to the publisher

FORWARD MOTION
On the Road
In Scooters and Wheelchairs

Contents

FORWARD MOTION
On the Road
In Scooters and Wheelchairs

Editor's Thanks

It is a powerful lesson in the interconnectedness of all creation to consider those I want to thank for making this book possible.

To begin with, Donald McNeil was my shining example and teacher of how to live fully with a less than fully functioning body. He was cheerful! He seemed to view the scooter as a form of liberation, not a constant reminder of what he could no longer do on his own. To him this book is dedicated with much love.

The people I interviewed created its substance, and I thank them heartily for all that they have taught and shared with me. Their stories will amaze you in their variety, practical ingenuity, openness, thoughtful insights, and humor. That they would talk to me at all is something of a wonder! Except for Jeff, they had never before laid eyes on me. They kept me going during the not-always-such-fun editing process—when I remembered it was their lives and stories I was working with. I realized that I couldn't stop.

I received much support from family and friends! They seemed to know what such an effort is about and gave me good suggestions, encouragement, critique—and occasionally a swift kick: sons Alec and Rick and daughter Mia; brothers Jim—the final editor—and David, and their wives Mary and Marina; coach Jeanne duPrau and her lively writing group; Trisha Clifford and Ginger Johnson. Jean Crawford and Marya and Lee Shahinian opened their homes to me for writing retreat days and weeks, in beautiful places away from home and distraction. Lee Shahinian, MD, checked the terms in the glossary for accuracy. Immense thanks to Malcolm White, who recently corrected almost half the proof!

Helping me stay a bit balanced during alternate periods of writing and procrastination were treasured friends from other parts of my life: Sally Anschel, Grace Azevedo, Diane Berman, Christine Chatwell, Jennie Curtis, Elaine Enos, Jodie Hines, Linda Hubly, Julie Jenkins, Grace Johnston, Rory Kaplan, Jane Kos, Jane Lewenthal, Alison Carpenter Lucas, Joan, Wally, and Lisa MacDonald, Nancy Nelson, Debi Peterman, Cam Thompson, and the participants at the discussions, retreats, and weekly meditations at the Insight Meditation Center of the Mid-Peninsula, and at Mercy Center in Burlingame.

Copy editor and college friend Marilyn Johnson reread the entire manuscript and made many useful corrections, most of which I include here. Remaining errors are not hers!

Behind and before any of these were my parents, Ruth and Jim Ottaway, who gave me life and love, a family of journalists, a fine education, and Dad's, "Just get on with it!" Mother taught me the psalms and was my first spiritual guide.

My foundation also rests in the lives, teachings, and living communities of Jesus Christ and Shakyamuni Buddha. Important for me in these realms have been Pastors Sam Little, Harold Brumbaum, Michael Rollie Jones, son Rick Sherer, Zen practitioner and teacher Yvonne Rand, and Father Tom Hand.

My children are spiritually rich and deep. Conversations over many years with them have been alive and insightful. More recently, Rick founded Berith Christian Fellowship in Oakland, California—a source of ongoing challenge and sustenance for me.

I feel profoundly blessed by each of you. Thank you from my deepest heart,

Ruth Sherer
San Mateo, CA
June 2008

FORWARD MOTION
On the Road
In Scooters and Wheelchairs

Introduction

The impetus for this book came from Donald McNeil, a dear friend and exuberant scooter user when he could no longer walk very far. After he died, I wanted to honor him in some way.

There were numerous other scooter and electric wheelchair users on the streets nearby. Seeing them tooling around, with varying degrees of confidence and enthusiasm, inspired me to interview some of them and to record and tell their stories.

Here is a reference resource of examples and possibilities for those who are considering or who already use scooters or electric wheelchairs, for their friends and families, and for the health professionals who work with them.

I have learned from these people and their stories the new freedom and options that these vehicles have added to their lives. Their lives did not need to be as restricted as they had been. They could get around on their own! They could even take them in cars, go on trips in planes!

We may all learn to enlarge our vision of what is possible in this life for people with limited mobility. I have been moved, astonished, and amused by the stories that are printed here.

These stories will offer a fresh view to those who may feel diminished by physical limitations, and a new perspective to those who view such people as diminished.

I hope that those who use or might use these vehicles, and their families and friends, will see and use some of the new approaches to life that are described in this book.

The book will give health care professionals another tool for encouraging their clients and offering them an added measure of freedom and range of possibilities in their lives.

I hope that all readers will be able to see people in scooters and wheelchairs with new eyes and fewer stereotypes.

I.

—

Meeting Donald McNeil

Donald McNeil
and
Ruth Sherer

Meeting Donald Mcneil

I met Donald McNeil in August of 1994 at the Santa Clara County Fair in San Jose, California. He was with old friends, and they had stopped at the fair booth where I was handing out information about child sexual abuse—a booth many shied away from. We chatted briefly, and they departed: he on his small golf-cart-like scooter, an electric vehicle used by increasing numbers of people who find it difficult to walk very far, his friends walking with him.

Several hours later, on my way out of the fairgrounds we met again—much to my surprise. Donald and his friends were having trouble getting the scooter seat off its base, which was necessary in order to raise it with an electric hoist into the trunk of the car. Without a second thought, and having no idea where they lived—or much about them at all—I said, "You can put it into the back of my truck without taking the seat off."

For some reason I assumed that the woman in Donald's group would accompany me back to Donald's house. Not so! Donald pulled himself up into the cab, along with a tank of oxygen he was toting. I was startled and a little alarmed at first, at the thought of driving this unknown man who-knew-where. Something in me decided that this was not a problem and off we went. His home turned out to be about four miles from mine.

Donald must have sensed my uncertainty about driving with him. He immediately began reassuring me about himself—a college

13

administrator who had lived in various places around the country, including Madison, Wisconsin, where my daughter had gone to school and lived at the time. He was also interested in my story and we had a genial conversation on the way home.

We arrived at Donald's home ahead of his friends and he showed me around his apartment. We sat and talked for a while, and he asked me whether I would like to get together again. I knew the answer was yes.

Thus began our relationship, which was to last a precious year and a half, and during which I came to feel a part of Donald's family. I was with him when his brother Jerry's wife died. His youngest son Andy was an intern and first-year resident at Stanford Hospital. I saw a number of his relatives and friends from over the years come to visit him. And we took trips together: to the coast, the city—San Francisco, the redwoods at Muir Woods, Mount Tamalpais, Point Reyes and Tomales Bay.

At the time I met him, Donald had survived lung cancer for twelve years. He had been coping with pulmonary fibrosis for several years. He took numerous medications, including steroids, which enhanced the quality of his life for some time but also had side effects resulting in the need for more medications.

Oxygen was a godsend. When at home, Donald could connect to one of a number of four–foot–high oxygen tanks that lined the living room. The tubing from the tank was about fifty feet long and allowed him to walk all over the apartment. When going out, he toted a smaller wheeled canister of oxygen, 'refueled' from one of the large oxygen tanks. These canisters could be loaded onto the scooter, and we took as many in the car as needed for the length of the journey.

When we visited a friend in the Central Valley, we didn't know how long we might be gone. We could see how much oxygen it took to get there, allow for the same amount to get home, and then stay and visit until the remaining tanks were emptied. Occasionally we ran a little short, but Donald could survive without the oxygen for a while if he just sat or reclined. And it never seemed to keep him home.

We spent several days on Tomales Bay for my birthday one year and Donald had a large tank of oxygen delivered to the place where we stayed. Wherever we went, he took his scooter and used it when walking any distance greater than about half a block. Of course the disease—pulmonary fibrosis—is progressive, so the distance Donald could walk, even with the oxygen, grew shorter over time. But we had almost a year and a half during which he really could and wanted to get out and do things.

Donald's scooter was the Sidekick model manufactured by Pride. It had three wheels, an upholstered seat with arm rests, controls on the handle bars, and a basket in front for jackets, Kleenex, binoculars—whatever the outing required. He used the scooter with a certain abandon and in all seasons. In the summer he liked to wear very short jeans shorts and colorful sport shirts: plaids, flowers, bright pink. In cooler weather, he favored khaki slacks with the shirts, various sweaters, his two-tone tan jacket and a plaid golf hat.

One of my fondest memories is of watching Donald get on his scooter. A wide smile would appear on his face, and he would jet off, leaving me holding my breath and saying a prayer for the people and things in his path. The scooter made him a free man again.

"Donald never did anything once," his daughter-in-law Dale joked, speaking of his marriages, his children and his work life. And there was a passion that wove its way throughout his life: a love of writing and history; an appreciation for the education he had received on the GI bill after World War II; and his desire to see that every American have the opportunity for a college education, whether they could afford it or not.

Donald had worked as an administrator within the Wisconsin, Maine, and California university systems; he lobbied to keep tuitions low, and to extend educational opportunity by television and computer to those who could not come to the campus. In promoting long-distance learning, he was ahead of his time. His conviction that public radio and television are essential cultural assets led him to serve on the board of the Corporation for Public Broadcasting and—practically single-handedly and at the end of his career—to found the public broadcasting archives at the University of Maryland.

Donald was a great and cheerful extrovert. He loved to see old friends and make new ones. He enjoyed meeting my friends and could keep a conversation genial with the most divergent of viewpoints, his being well to the left of center. I remember his talking with the rather conservative husband of a friend of mine; it was a vigorous discussion, but totally without rancor, to the credit of them both.

Donald kept in close touch with distant family and friends on the computer—his mistress, I teased him, because it provided me such great competition for his attention. Often when I arrived to do something with him, he would be sitting at the computer, reading and writing letters, enjoying thoroughly this ease in connecting with friends far and near.

We had met at the movies by chance not long after our initial meeting at the fairgrounds, and we continued to see films together, go out for dinner, take the scooter to the park for a spin and some exercise for me, and perhaps a picnic for both of us. It was particularly lovely to pull up beach chairs in the late afternoon light on a grassy mound overlooking a marsh and watch shorebirds like ducks and egrets come to nest in the evening. At home, we enjoyed doing the daily crossword puzzle in the newspaper together. When we completed it, Donald said that between us, we knew everything.

Late in the evening, he would occasionally have anxiety attacks, despite the medication he took for it. His solution was to go for a drive. It seemed to relieve the tension and fear. We would use my truck, get on the freeway, speed along in the dark with all the city lights illuminating the sky. And we'd have a good time talking and enjoying the sights in town and country—sights that he hadn't always seen before, since he had moved from Washington, DC to California just a few months before I met him. Somehow en route, we often stopped for ice cream—a favorite of his.

Until the last few months of his life, nothing kept Donald from enjoying life to the full. With each small crisis he would lose a little steam, a little joie de vivre. But after a bit of time he would recover, adjust to his new level of capability, and enjoy life again. He seemed to feel that his cup was at least half full, his difficulty breathing a challenge to his creativity and ingenuity.

After Christmas 1996, however, his joy in living seemed to ebb away, day by day. He made a tremendous effort to come to my sixtieth birthday party the following February third. But after that, he wanted to have hospice help at home. Until that time, he had taken pleasure in the doctor's declining to recommend it for him; it meant he had more time. But now he was ready, even looking forward to peace and the end. He was uncomfortable, each day and night seemed to require tremendous effort. We did whatever possible to make him comfortable.

Midpeninsula Hospice came regularly and at odd times when needed, for nursing and personal care and support. Women from Chariot of Fire, an alcohol and drug rehabilitation program for women coming out of jail, cleaned, cooked, cared for, and above all, loved him. They were with him during the day; I was with him at night.

The morning of March 8, 1996, Donald slipped into unconsciousness. He died that evening. He wanted to go with dignity and at home. He did. I loved him.

After the burial in Portland, Oregon, where he grew up, there was a memorial celebration "at the beach," as he called Shoreline Park in Mountain View where we often went for walks and lunch. Family and friends came from around the country. People spoke of memorable times with him, his loving and mentoring influence in their lives. His son Andy showed slides of Donald's life, beginning with a picture of him in his mother's arms.

The final slide showed Donald on his scooter (shown on the front cover). This felt like an emblem of our happiest and most adventurous times together. It floated in my mind. More and more, I noticed people on scooters, three-wheel bicycles, and electric wheelchairs—tooling around town on their own. The images began to blend together, then form a book—in honor and memory of Donald.

One day in August 1996, five months after Donald's death, I

saw a woman in Mountain View using a scooter on the Whisman Avenue overpass. I stopped my truck and ran after her. She was Peggy Madden, and she couldn't imagine what she could do for anyone else in her predicament with a broken leg. I explained that I wanted to write a book in Donald's memory—about other people who use scooters and electric wheelchairs to get out and about. She agreed to an interview, and that was the beginning of this book.

II.

Accidents

Jeff: "Whatever State You Want"

Peggy: Stuck at Home; But Not for Long

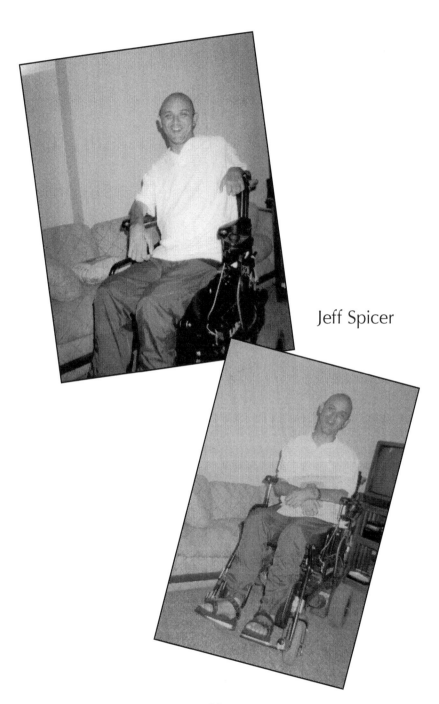

Jeff Spicer

Jeff Spicer

**"I just wasn't going to be depressed about the injury.
I didn't have to be; I didn't want to be."**

On a warm August day in 1991, graduate student Jeff Spicer and several friends set off on their annual canoe trip down the Wisconsin River. As they paddled along, they spotted a basketball hoop nailed to a tree, there in the middle of nowhere. They angled their canoes into the bank, grabbed the volleyball they had brought along, and started a game of 'horse.' With one man perched atop another's shoulders, the two teams vied for points, shooting at the basketball hoop.

At the end of the game, when the others ducked into the woods to relieve themselves, Jeff decided to go for a swim. He waded in about knee deep and dove forward—and went head first into an underwater sandbar.

"I think I was conscious for about thirty seconds," Jeff recalls. "I remember seeing my contacts floating down the river and thinking, 'I can't move.' I was paralyzed and face down in the water—like a dead man's float. I couldn't push myself over to breathe."

When Jeff's friends returned and saw him, they were amused at first. "They thought I was joking—lying there in the water—because

21

I was a strong, competitive swimmer, and I was in great shape."
When they pulled Jeff out of the water, he was purple, bloated,
and not breathing. One of them administered CPR and got him
breathing again, but they didn't know what to do after that.

Almost unbelievably, a doctor came canoeing down the river. He
stopped and helped get Jeff stabilized. One of his buddies canoed
down the river to the nearest farmhouse and called 911. There
weren't any roads at the site of the accident, so the rescue team had
to send a boat in. They strapped Jeff onto a stretcher board, paddled
him to a road head, and finally got him on a helicopter and back to
the University of Wisconsin Hospital in Madison. He was uncon-
scious the entire time.

The medical team at the hospital found that Jeff had injured his
spinal cord between the fifth and sixth cervical vertebrae in his
neck. He was paralyzed in his lower body and much of his upper
body. He still had some use of his arms and hands, however, so he
would be able to eat and write—and use a joy stick to control his
electric wheelchair—though that would come later.

Jeff then spent the next five months in rehab at the university
hospital. "I had great support from my parents, my sisters and
brothers, and everyone I knew," he said. "Over two–hundred people
visited me while I was in the hospital: fraternity friends from under-
graduate days and many friends I had met in graduate school. They
would sneak tacos to me in the hospital, and they sneaked me out of
the hospital several times. One of them even dropped off his twenty-
inch color TV for me to use!" One night nearly his whole fraternity
showed up: over forty guys completely filled the room.

Many athletic young men injured so badly early in life would be
bitter or depressed, but that was not Jeff's reaction. "There seems
to be a perception that after an injury a person's disposition and
attitude are influenced heavily by the new situation," he says. "My
experience has been just the opposite: to some degree, whatever
happens after a traumatic injury, people are the same people they
were before. With friends of mine who are suddenly in wheelchairs,
their attitudes toward life haven't changed that much.

"I just wasn't going to be depressed about the injury. I didn't have to be; I didn't want to be. I don't see a need for being depressed. You put yourself into whatever state you want to be in. If some people choose to be unhappy about their situations, maybe that's more positive in the long run for them, but that is not what works for me."

Now in a wheelchair, Jeff was released from the hospital just before Christmas of 1991 and went home to Milwaukee for about three weeks with his parents. Then he moved into an apartment in Madison and returned to graduate school at the University.

"I was working on a master's degree in real estate, appraisal, and investment analysis," Jeff says. "The highly regarded former chairman of the real estate program was Dr. James Graascamp. He had polio when he was younger and was a quadriplegic, in a wheelchair his entire adult life. So I had an excellent model for what was possible. His example made it easier for me to go back into the program; and the professors were all understanding."

Jeff's first wheelchair was a manual one. A power chair—"You don't like to call it an electric chair," he remarks wryly—was delivered later. It was "a real behemoth," and barely fit through the apartment door. When he sat in it, he felt "contained in a large box," as though the chair was encompassing him, rather than being a functional part of him. Jeff describes learning to use a wheelchair as a process of understanding over time how to integrate his body into the wheelchair, making it a part of the body and using it with that kind of ease.

In graduate school, Jeff had his first—of many—wheelchair travel adventures. He and several other students traveled with a professor to Eastern Europe after Communism fell apart, to study the effects of privatization on the real estate markets there.

"It was a fascinating trip," Jeff recalls, "but the area is completely inaccessible to wheelchair users. I couldn't take the power chair because the electric currents differ from place to place and we were in a number of cities: Moscow, St. Petersburg, Prague, Warsaw, and Budapest. For the most part there were cobblestone streets and sidewalks, and the concept of a curb cut was foreign to most of them. So I was in a manual chair, a very nice, lightweight model, a Quicky

GPV. The back folds down and the wheels pop off with a quick release."

Even in a smaller manual chair, Jeff found that doorways and elevator doors were not always very wide. "My friends would take the wheels off the chair, and one of them would take a deep breath and pull me into a tiny, tiny elevator—almost on top of him. Two of the others would run up the stairs with the wheels to meet us. Meanwhile the person with me in the elevator is just dying, holding me up until we get to the top. We'd meet the other guys, put the wheels back on, and away we'd go," he laughed appreciatively as he remembered his friends helping him through such obstacles.

The group saw few other people in wheelchairs. "I thought one woman was going to break her neck staring at me," Jeff says. "We were all dressed in suits and ties because we were going to talk with city planners and leaders. My friends were hopping me down the stairs into the Paris Metro (subway) and the woman turned around to watch while she walked down the stairs backwards carrying a big bag. I thought for sure she was going to fall!" Then in St. Petersburg, a woman came up to Jeff outside a church, wailing, hugging, and kissing him and 'shooting' her rosary beads at him.

In December 1993, soon after the trip to Eastern Europe, Jeff finished his master's degree. He then took some time off to do a weight-training program, build a lot more upper body strength, relax a bit, and start looking for a job. Eight months later, after a difficult search, he took a position as real estate development officer with the Madison Development Corporation. He would work there for about three years, helping them fulfill their mission to provide affordable housing and economic development in Madison.

Jeff's first "behemoth" power chair has since been replaced by an Action Arrow model made by Store, which better suits his needs and abilities. It has a battery-driven base with a separate seating system by LaBac that can recline, so he can shift his weight and adjust his position.

The Action Arrow goes about twenty miles between charges, depending on the terrain. "But of course," Jeff says, "if you recline up and down all day, that alone can drain the battery." There are some things he would like to change about this chair, like having it closer to the ground for a safer center of gravity, or having one foot plate instead of two for greater comfort, but he is philosophical about it: "Sometimes you have to choose between comfort and safety.

"I truck around in this chair in the wintertime as well as in warmer weather. One winter day I was on Bascom Hill, a large, fairly steep hill that leads up to the main building on the university campus. It had just started snowing, and there was ice under the snow. To get to class I had to go down Bascom Hill. As I descended I had the chair in full reverse gear, but I kept sliding downhill."

At that point, Jeff decided that his best option was to run into a tree—which he did, though his feet were pushed almost under the wheels of the chair. "Luckily I didn't get hurt and three large guys stopped to help. I had one person on each side and another behind me—making sure I wouldn't go anywhere and holding the armrests. We got back onto the sidewalk and, with the chair still in full reverse gear, these guys steered me down the hill, almost like a team of sled dogs.

"The only time I've ever been hurt wasn't because of the power wheelchair. I was in the manual chair at a wedding, and some friends wanted to push me outside to take pictures. The front of the wheelchair caught on a step, the chair tipped forward, and the guy pushing the chair just unloaded me like a dump-truck dumping its load.

"There I was, flying forward with no hope of bracing myself to break the fall. After I landed and was sprawled out on the ground, my friends were all silent for a minute, fearing something terrible had happened to me. Finally I said, 'Hey! Pick me up! There's nothing wrong. Just pick me up!' I just got a big scrape on my forehead. It was bleeding a little bit, but we got pictures despite the incident. Later that night, we actually had a good laugh over it."

Health insurance will often pay for wheelchairs. As a back-up when private insurance reaches its cap, the federal government's Medical Assistance Program allows one chair every five years—

for people on Supplemental Security Income or Social Security Disability Income.

Jeff has attendants through State Medical Assistance and sometimes they are in short supply. "Part of this is because the unemployment rate is so low; you can do better working for MacDonald's." They do not know in advance that they may be able to travel to Eastern Europe or places like Atlanta, Tampa, Phoenix, and Miami.

Jeff gets help in two short shifts, morning and night. An attendant helps him get dressed, have breakfast, and get ready for work in the morning. Jeff rolls the wheelchair to work himself or sometimes takes the bus. As he learned on Bascom Hill, it can be hard to handle in the snow and ice. In the evening an attendant comes to help him with dinner, do some cleaning, and help him get to bed. Attendants often become friends: "You ride this fine line between being friends with people and having them as workers."

Jeff's job in real estate requires that he go out and look at sites and neighborhoods. So being able to get there is crucial. As he puts it, "I can't just take the bus and ask the driver to detour so I can get the flavor of the neighborhood." After proving that he needed a van to do his job, he found that if he bought one, the state department of Vocational Rehabilitation would pay for the modifications necessary for him to drive it. One adaptation that was made was installing a peg underneath the wheelchair that connects to a floor–locking system in his van. This holds the chair in place in the van.

"When I first got the van, one of my attendants and her boyfriend and I decided we'd go for a shakedown cruise to Pensacola, Florida and then on to Miami. We spent Thanksgiving week traveling around in the warm areas. It was thirty degrees here in Madison and about seventy–five or eighty in Miami." The three travelers sat outside by a pool and visited with the attendant's relatives and friends. And Jeff interviewed for jobs.

Being dependent on the state for services involves other considerations. Aside from a home and van, you cannot have more than two thousand dollars in assets. So saving much money is not possible, and it is difficult to become gradually less dependent.

"My goal is to be independent financially," says Jeff, "and I think

I will achieve this goal in the near future. I now have enough income and career experience to be paid quite a bit more. I envision working as a real estate analyst or portfolio manager, something I like doing because if you manage appropriately it provides quality for the neighborhood."

Jeff would also like to live in a warm area of the country; he finds the cost of living in the South is more reasonable, too. However, the logistics of moving are difficult. "I've had some phone interviews, but people just aren't interested until you're in town," Jeff says. "Also, I realize that whenever I move, I'm not going to get the same kind of assistance that I receive in Wisconsin.

"Being physically dependent on other people and devices will always be part of my life and is something I got used to relatively quickly. Of course it can be frustrating at times. One of the especially frustrating things for me is my inability to bend over and pick something up off the floor. I have someone here when I wake up, when I go to the bathroom, when I go to the shower, when I go to bed at night. That can be a bit trying.

"Sometimes you have to almost disassociate yourself as you are getting assistance with very personal everyday life functions. Your private time can be lacking. But you don't have to let that dependence bother you unless you want to. My life does not seem that different from the average person's everyday life. Mentally and emotionally my life is just like everyone else's.

"Eventually I would like to have an able–bodied roommate again. I haven't had one for probably three years and that can be helpful. If the attendant doesn't show up, someone is there who can fill in temporarily."

Jeff has an amazing capacity for taking the bad with the good. "Every day is an adventure," he says, "and I do manage on my own at times. One night I had been out late with a friend and decided to sleep reclined in my wheelchair—it was too late to expect an attendant to come toss me into bed. As I was trying to grab my pillow so I could lean back and sleep, I knocked the armrest off the bar that it floated on. As I reached over to pull it up, I slipped, fell onto my side, and could not pull myself back up to a sitting position. So from one or two in the morning until my attendant arrived about eight o'clock, I was stuck lying chest down on this bar. The worst part was that all the lights were on and I was facing a clock, watching the time tick by. It was a distressing experience and very painful wedged between the back of the chair and this metal bar—kind of rough on the ribs. I had a huge welt on my side from lying there for several hours. I didn't have a cell phone so I had no way to call for help. But with each experience like this, you learn a valuable lesson.

"I've had some health problems—episodes of high blood pressure and bladder infections, but I like to have a positive outlook. You can look at life in two ways. You can sit around and be grumpy and unhappy about your situation and have no friends. I don't choose to live that way. The more positive I am, the more people I meet, the more friends I have, the greater I think my life is. I don't see my life as all that bad. Some people ask me how I deal with it all. It's just natural. You do what you have to do."

Since I interviewed Jeff, he has moved to Florida, married, found a job, and had children! He and his friends still sometimes dream that he can stand and walk. Who's to say what is possible?

Peggy Madden

"It all happened on the Fourth of July weekend. I went biking and swimming that day, and I just decided to see if I could still roller skate!"

Seeing Peggy Madden using a scooter inspired me to begin this book. She was on the Whisman Avenue overpass in Mountain View, California when I saw her, stopped my truck, and ran to catch up with her. Most people need a scooter because of some chronic problem; but she had been in a skating accident and was only in a cast temporarily. We did not know each other, but she agreed to an interview.

"I have been renting a scooter because I broke my leg about six weeks ago while I was out roller skating," said Peggy, a lively woman in her thirties. "It all happened on the Fourth of July weekend. I went biking and swimming that day, and I just decided to see if I could still roller skate!"

Parking her car, Peggy started skating around the parking lot at one of the nearby computer companies. Something caught under a wheel and she started falling. "I heard a snap and it didn't sound good. I was out in the middle of this Sunday afternoon with nobody around. How could I get back to my car? How could I drive? It was also quite painful.

"I crawled to the car keys that had gone flying; and I kind of 'scootched' my way out of the parking lot. The pavement was real hot. On my hands and knees, I started down the street. Cars came by, but they didn't stop."

There was one house next to the parking lot where Peggy had fallen; there were cars in the driveway. When Peggy got there, she sat down, and a lady came out of the house and asked if she needed help. Peggy thought she might need an ambulance.

The woman, who said she was a nurse, returned with an Ace bandage, pillows, and an ice pack, and propped up Peggy's leg. She called an ambulance and Peggy was taken to Valley Medical Center.

Peggy had multiple fractures in her leg. "I begged the doctor, 'Don't say the surgery word!' But he said it probably would be better in the long run. Otherwise, I might have arthritis later on." Surgery would pin this all together with four little tiny screws and that should hold the ankle and leg together. (As it turned out, they put in a plate and eight screws).

The doctor insisted that Peggy get the swelling down before he could operate. But she got bored at home with her foot elevated, and she started vacuuming and washing floors—so the swelling didn't go down very fast. Although she broke her leg on July seventh, she didn't have surgery until the eighteenth; but the surgery went well. In the recovery room the nurse told Peggy that as soon as she could wiggle her toes, she could go to a hospital bed.

Four hours later, when she still had no feeling in either leg, she started to panic. The anesthetist came back to reassure her, and she was transferred to a hospital bed. Finally a few hours later, she had begun to wiggle her toes; feeling returned little by little—and then throbbing. The doctor gave her morphine intravenously; when she needed more, she could press a lever and a dose would be released every so often—enough to kill the pain.

The next morning in came the therapist who said, "Okay, let's start walking." Peggy hadn't gotten up at all and couldn't see how she could start walking. She didn't feel comfortable on crutches; but she had a walker and used it then and in the afternoon, with the aid of the therapist.

"Then for the first time I finally got a little rest. When I opened my eyes, there were four nurses standing at the end of my bed. One was saying, 'We think you're ready to go home.' According to them, even if doctors say you can stay overnight, when the administrators feel that you're strong enough to go home, you go home—or else you start paying out of your own pocket, even though it's a county hospital. Fortunately a girl at work was willing to take me home.

"I had other help too," Peggy continued. "At the Adventist church I go to, we have a volunteer Church Care program. Every Sabbath someone comes and takes me to church, and they helped with grocery shopping, and getting the mail.

"I live by myself and don't have family here in California, but I hate to depend on anybody. I thought there must be a way to get around town without having to rely on bus stops and people hauling me up and down."

Peggy called the Palo Alto Orthopedic Company to rent a scooter. She had come home from the hospital on July nineteenth, but the scooter was not available until the twenty-third. "On that day, believe me, I called and said, 'Even if it doesn't have a full battery, I'll plug it in at my own house. Just give me that thing! I want to get out of here!'

"They delivered it and put a ramp at the door. They charge $150 a month for the scooter and it's well worth it! Just to have my independence and get out. The scooter I use is quite small, and it gets right into my office. I can scoot around the counters and go to my desk. I've had this Amigo scooter for about six weeks. I can go an hour and a half and then turn it around and come back. I don't know what I'd do without it. I can't drive a car, but I can take the scooter downtown—to the mailbox and the bank, to get photos, and there's the Farmers Market on Sunday. I've just had a blast with this thing."

Some years before the accident, Peggy was transferred from Minneapolis to California by her employer. "After years of teaching computers and computer structures to the hardware guys, I was so bored I thought if I saw another bit or byte I'd scream!"

She decided on a job in government and found a "way in the door" with a clerk/typist position in the County Probation Department. "I thought that would really be interesting. I'd never been in a jail before; I'd never seen or met anybody who went to one."

Since Peggy has a bachelor's degree, eventually she would like to move into a better position, perhaps as a public defender investigator. "They interview inmates; they go home at five. I'll just keep taking different tests as they come along. And if something matches, fine. If it doesn't, this job is close to home and it's paying the bills."

After recovering from the surgery, Peggy started back to work— at first for only four hours a day, then full time. It was about a mile and a half from her home on the scooter and took about thirty minutes at five miles an hour. By comparison, walking takes about twenty minutes. "I'm in the fresh air and get to see what's going on around me," Peggy adds. "I say hi to everybody and they seem really friendly."

When Peggy went back to the doctor to get a walking cast, she asked to see the x-ray. "You couldn't even see the breaks on the x-ray anymore!" The doctor said that in about a year she could have the plate and screws removed if she wished; otherwise she could leave them in place if they didn't bother her. She also wondered if the leg would be shriveled up to nothing when the cast came off, if she would still need the scooter, and whether it would be painful getting the leg back to normal strength.

Peggy then spoke of one of her more daring adventures on the scooter. "The first time I took the scooter any distance, I went to get some groceries. You have to cross six lanes on El Camino to get there. I thought, 'Do I want to cross El Camino? Even if I press that little button to change the lights, will that give me enough time to go across six lanes?' I was just nervous. But I juiced up the scooter and said, 'Okay, let's give it a whirl.'

"It was a beautiful sunny day. About halfway to El Camino, the scooter just stopped. I pressed the accelerator again and it went ahead. I thought, 'What if it does this going <u>across</u> El Camino?' It kind of scared me, it was going so slowly. But it kept going and I made it across the six lanes.

"In the store, I got a basket and put it on the floor of the scooter. I can carry about two grocery bags. I even brought some bungy cord so nothing would fall out on the way back.

"On the way back, I set out toward home and those six lanes again. I felt more nervous as I got to the corner. I pulled up to stop—and the whole steering rod came right out of the handle bar! I couldn't go forward. I couldn't go backward. Now what should I do? Here I was a cripple with a broken leg. What a predicament! I couldn't even find a pay phone. And cars were just whoosh, whooshing by. I sat there for ten minutes.

"'Well Lord,' I said finally, 'how do I get out of this one? You're gunna have to tell me. I have no idea.' So, I put the rod back into the handle bar and tried it one more time. It moved just a little bit—there was still juice in this thing and a connection somehow.

"I waited for the light to turn green. When I got to the traffic island in the middle of the street, the light turned red. I was afraid if I stopped, I wouldn't be able to start again. So I just slowed down and braced my foot on the ground to stop it. When the light finally turned green, I pushed off, and I made it across to the other side and most of the way home. I got to within one foot of my front door when the scooter completely died."

The man who rented Peggy the scooter said the whole thing was broken, and he took it back to his shop. The rod had just snapped in half and had to be welded back together.

"I thought, The good Lord has angels up there. Who else got me from El Camino to within a foot of my front door. That's about the biggest miracle I've ever seen!"

III.

Beginners...and Pros

Dorothy: Getting Started

Cheryl: "Don't Hesitate"

Almira: Lap of Luxury

Dorothy Brioza

Dorothy Brioza

**"I can take a wheelchair...
(but) it's more fun in the scooter!"**

Dorothy Brioza is a relatively new scooter user. She lives with her husband Ernie in a mobile home park in Sunnyvale, California, and was referred to me by her neighbor Kay Heller, whose story also appears in this book.

Particularly this last year, Dorothy has had trouble walking because of arthritis in her knees and back. "I'm just going along the best I can," she told me. "We got a scooter and it has made a big difference. I ride around the trailer park and I use it at the clubhouse all the time. I like my scooter. It's fun!"

Dorothy's interests are centered mainly around the trailer park. She and Ernie have lived there about fourteen years, and most of their friends live there as well. "The people here are really great," she continued, "and we seem to cling to each other. The whole park rallies to support each other. Especially the ones that have been here for years, since we know each other so well.

"This morning we heard that one of our very good friends just passed away, and that kind of hit me in the stomach. That's what you have to expect in a place like this; we are all getting older. I find myself becoming hardened to it all—as much as I can. My husband sometimes thinks he would like to get out of here. I told him that it is no better anywhere else. It's part of our life."

Dorothy and Ernie started looking at scooters when a salesman came to their house to show them one made by Lark. Dorothy liked its compactness, but wanted something with a cover over the batteries. After she had test-driven both the Lark and the Pride brands, they finally settled on a small scooter made by Pride, the Sidekick, which does have a battery cover.

"I love my Pride," Dorothy laughs. "I think I will use the scooter more this summer. I would like to take it out of the trailer park and go shopping, but I would have to go too far and there is an awful lot of traffic. We are trying to find a flag for it—to give it some identity and more visibility.

"I try to take the scooter out every day. I miss not doing it. Using the scooter is my walk! When I first came out with it though, I had more attention than I really wanted. I was a little self-conscious about it. But everybody was surprised and glad to see that I was getting the help I needed. It gives me a little more independence."

There are electric lifts available that enable people to connect the scooter to a hoist, raise the scooter up into the air, and swing it around into the trunk of a car or the back of a van with a remote control.

"If I get a lift," Dorothy points out, "then I can take the scooter wherever I go. We are looking into getting one, but I don't know yet what my husband will do. With a lift I could just leave the scooter in the car and use it without my husband having to come with me. I would like to become more independent with the scooter."

Dorothy also speaks of the reality of going places that only appear to be accessible to wheelchairs and scooters. "At the clubhouse there is a ramp from the street. But when you get to the clubhouse door, they don't have any way for you to open it. You just go on a wing and a prayer! But I manage. Going in isn't too bad. And inside the clubhouse it's clear sailing—all level floors. But going out it's always with a bang—you are coming off more of a bump going out. I'm just hoping it won't do any harm."

It is important to Dorothy to be able to access the clubhouse since she enjoys the social life there. Every Thursday she plays canasta with friends, and there are coffee klatches daily. She says there are people at the clubhouse every day, a very active group of park residents and friends.

Around the house, Dorothy does not use the scooter, her walker or wheelchair, or even her cane. "I have trouble getting around, but I have my own speed when I'm on my own!" When she is in the house, there is usually something nearby to hold onto if needed.

"Today I cooked a pot of soup here at home, and we will have that for our dinner tonight," Dorothy continues. "My husband helps in the kitchen, and we manage together. But I don't cook or entertain the way we used to. I loved having company for dinner. Once in a while I do it now, but it's hard.

"When I go into the drugstore, I have to walk too, since they don't have a scooter or a wheelchair for you to use. I use the shopping cart for support. There are people a lot worse off than I am; I'm not completely handicapped."

Dorothy has two children. Her son has two boys, and he and his wife live in nearby Fremont. Her daughter and her husband Eric and his eleven-year-old son, Justin, live in the Sierra Nevada mountains in Truckee, California. Occasionally, they come down to visit her and Ernie for a weekend. Dorothy hoped Justin would get a big kick out of the scooter. "Unfortunately," she said, "the last time they came, it was raining like the dickens so we didn't take the scooter out and he never got to see it. I know he would love to get his hands on it!

"When I ride around in the markets, kids point out the scooter to their mothers. They come over and ask me questions: What's that? Why do you use it? I explain that to them. One kid asked me if he could have a ride. I put him on my lap and took him around the store. He was a little thing. It was cute. One of the kids wanted to drive it himself. I had to say no to that!

"One time we took the scooter in the car to Reno. We had to take it apart. I think there are four or five different parts you can take off. It's very easy to lift each part. And Ernie assembles it in one, two, three minutes flat. Nothing to it!

"When we got to Reno, we stayed at one of the combined hotel-casinos, a beautiful place and ideal for a scooter since you have clear sailing all the way through." At the hotel-casino, there are no stairs and no need to go outside—making getting around there smooth and easy.

Dorothy and Ernie also took the scooter on a cruise. When they had to change planes it was a bit cumbersome, but the scooter was fine on the ship. "I had all my independence and I was able to go anywhere I pleased. You do have to wait for someone to open the door because you can't drive and open the door at the same time. The elevators on this ship weren't particularly large either. With me and that scooter in it, that was about it!

"We are going again to Alaska in June. I want to take the scooter with me, but I have to leave this up to my husband. If we don't take it, I can take a wheelchair, but my arms get too tired using the wheelchair. Since I use it only when we go to a mall, I don't get strong enough to use it easily. It's more fun in the scooter!"

Cheryl Nafzgar

Cheryl Nafzgar

**"Don't hesitate to get a scooter if you can't get around well.
It will definitely change your life."**

It was a warm September day when I first met Cheryl Nafzgar jauntily navigating her scooter among the booths at a street fair in Palo Alto, California. As was my habit, I described to her the book I wanted to write about scooter users. She agreed to an interview later in her home.

"I guess I've had my scooter about two and a half years," she began. "Before that I had a very difficult time going any distance. I relied on my husband a lot to shop. We had to move very slowly because he was always afraid I was going to fall, and he would brace himself in case I did fall. So it was better for both of us after I got the scooter. He could walk normally, and I could not only keep up with him, I could go faster. I can now out-shop him!

"It's really made my life somewhat normal again to be able to get around. I've had the slow, progressive form of multiple sclerosis (MS) for eighteen years. The first twelve to fifteen years I didn't have anything wrong that you could see. Then it started to affect my walking. That's when I decided to get the scooter. And it makes a big difference. We've even put it on airplanes and flown it to Florida."

MS forces people to slow down. It sometimes takes Cheryl twice as long to do things as it used to to do things. Although she always used to be on time, now she has to allow for her slower pace and the fact that she must sometimes get the scooter out of the van. "Once I've gotten it out," she continued, "I can move a lot faster than I could walk, so that's good! But MS in general tires you. I find myself really exhausted sometimes when I wouldn't have been five years ago. Heat is the worst. It slows all your reactions even more than when it's cooler. So you just can't move when it's hot.

"Having to slow down is probably the hardest thing for me. Not being able to do everything I want to do. When I was able, I did a lot of physical stuff I can no longer do. Like woodworking. I built the living room couch. Things like that. Fortunately I was never a piano player or a tennis player! That I haven't had to give up."

Cheryl spoke fondly of their fourteen–year–old son—still at home—who facilitates her getting around. "He's a big help," Cheryl continued a little nostalgically. "If it's really hot and I don't want to spend five minutes in the sun getting the scooter out, he does that for me. I don't know what I'll do when he goes off to college!"

Cheryl does enjoy cooking and has a big family—including five children she has raised and a couple of others the family has taken in. "I like to entertain and I still do a lot of that," she said. "My husband just turned 60 this year, so we had a big party for him. I don't use my scooter when I'm cooking. I just use my cane."

The scooter has helped Cheryl go longer distances. She has a Sun Dancer, made by Pride, that she bought from a man who drove a couple of hours from Sacramento with a big van full of scooters. She chose the smallest one. "It was candy apple red," Cheryl remembered, "so I thought it was kind of cheery; a little spunkier than the big four-wheeled gray ones. Mine is only a three–wheeler. I can get in and out of places a lot easier than I could with the bigger ones. I use it only for outdoor things—mall crawling is what I call it. Or doing fairs, going to the park, taking the dogs for a walk."

The dogs are two pugs, Sweet Pea and Sam, who love to ride in the scooter. "We went out to Stanford campus last weekend, and they fought over who was going to get to ride on it," Cheryl laughed, recalling the two scamps vying for position on her scooter. "There isn't room for both of them. They're not too large, but they're heavy and bulky. Sammy, the fat one, gets to ride most often because he hates to exercise. But that day I took Sweet Pea, the skinny one, on the floor board. Sammy needed to exercise and work off a little weight. We did circles around the quad, with Sammy running along trying to catch up with us."

The dogs may want to sit down and move more slowly, but Cheryl sometimes has the opposite problem: trying to move too fast.

"I've always moved fast. That's probably how I broke my finger— going too fast on the scooter. Last Christmas I was shopping in Macys. We were going to a party that night, so I had run out to get stockings. They had just started to put up a display and there were boxes all over one of the aisles.

"I was trying to get around this barricade, when I backed up and ran into some kind of a display, caught my finger, and broke it. Everybody came out of the woodwork to help. They got the fire department and the paramedics. I said, 'You know, I just have a broken finger. If you can drive me over to Stanford Hospital, I don't need to go in an ambulance.' They said, 'Oh no.' I guess they didn't want to be liable for anything.

"I couldn't drive my scooter to the emergency room to have my finger set, but I drove it back to the parking place and put it in the van. My finger didn't hurt, but I knew it was broken because it was bent out of alignment.

"In addition to shopping adventures, I use the scooter going to the movies, which we do a lot. I take it inside the movie theater and park it against the wall. I was leaving it outside, but I found that kids wanted to play with it. A couple of times I came out, and it was moved. I could tell that people had been messing with it.

"Another time in Macys, I parked the scooter and got out to go look at something; it was easier than trying to drive through the racks of clothes. A couple of little boys came along. I'd left my key in the scooter and they decided to take it for a ride! Little boys love it!

"They were probably seven and nine or so. Their mom came along and made them stop, but they were having a good time. Little boys always come up to me and say, 'How fast does it go? Can I drive it?' A lot of the time I let them. If they're real little, I put them on my lap and take them for a ride. We have two- and four-year-old grandkids of my husband's in Florida. I took them to the zoo with the scooter, and they liked riding it there.

"I also take the scooter on vacation. The only problem is that when I get there, since it weighs a hundred and fifty pounds, I need a couple of guys along to help—either put it into a van or break it down into three parts. And it's hard to break down. When I'm here at home, all I have to do is open up the back of my van and use the lift. A little arm comes out by remote control, and we just hook the scooter onto it and swing it into the van. It's wonderful...state of the art!" (See snapshot on page 42.)

Cheryl notices that the reactions of others when she is on the scooter are often not what one would expect. She reflected, "It seems people are really receptive or...just don't want to deal with me. Maybe it's just how I'm perceiving it. I don't know. People either go overboard helping me or they just want to get out of my way and not even see that I'm sitting there waiting for a door to be opened—as if I'm invisible.

"On the other hand, it's amazing how people stop me and ask where I got the scooter, or if they can rent one because their parents are coming to town. For whatever reason, you slow down, you begin to look at all the things that could be done to help people who can't get around so easily."

One thing many people in scooters or wheelchairs or even strollers become very aware of is the reality of walking up to a store where there is a handicapped placard in the window. This may mean only that there is a rail in the bathroom—if you can find your way to the bathroom. It doesn't necessarily mean there are wider aisles or that you can get through the bathroom door without someone else's assistance.

"The Americans with Disabilities Act (ADA) has certainly changed some things," Cheryl says. But as in many situations of attempting to follow the law, or to make shopping easier, or even in a genuine attempt to help others, making public places completely accessible involves more than a gesture here or there. It requires a comprehensive and well thought out plan, together with its implementation.

"I'm glad when I see a store that has automatic doors," Cheryl continued. "As soon as you step in front of it, it opens up. You don't have to sit there in the rain waiting for somebody to come along and open the door for you! Curb cutouts are great too.

"There are handicapped sections in most theaters now," Cheryl pointed out. "The seats are usually very good, at a reduced rate, and on the ground level where you can come into the orchestra section. If you had not been handicapped you might have bought seats up in the nosebleed section for ten dollars! Plus you often get good parking and you can usually take one person with you.

"Quite apart from the ADA or other laws, there are a lot of MS support groups. I've never gotten involved in one of those, but I volunteered at the MS Society in Santa Clara for a while. And I do see a lot of scooter people. Don't hesitate to get a scooter if you can't get around well. It will definitely change your life.

"One lady I know does everything in her scooter, including her grocery shopping. One time the two of us met for coffee in our scooters. It's probably a mile between our houses, and I had never experienced going that far. We ended up riding in the middle of a street because the sidewalk was too narrow for both of us. That was quite a sight to see, two scooters going down the middle of the street. We had a good time!"

Almira Bell

Almira Bell

"I've got every pleasure conceivable here and beauty is something I admire. So right now, you could say I'm living in the lap of luxury."

This interview with Almira "Jerry" Bell took place in her Mountain View, California apartment on a fine spring day. She was sitting in the living room in her manual wheelchair (she also has a scooter). Her apartment is on an inside corner of the senior housing complex where she lives. Many apartments, including Almira's, have a sliding glass door opening onto a large interior courtyard. Almira described how she came to live here. Her gratitude and appreciation for what she has struck me in sharp contrast with many who live here in Silicon Valley.

"I was raised in the Central Valley where we were migrant workers. My Dad couldn't read or write. A lot of times he had just enough gas to go a short distance to look for a job. They had my sister in Bakersfield and when they got to Fresno they had me. They couldn't move me around because I was just hardly staying alive on them. So they settled in Fresno. (As a child, Almira was in fragile health.)

"A factory where they made cottonseed oil was built right across the road. Mother taught Dad to write his own name and enough reading so he could get by. That's how he was able to work at the factory the thirteen years before he died. Other than that all we did was pick cotton, going out before it was light and working until it was dark.

"My momma was good. When I was about three years old, I'd toddle along in the field behind her. If I got ahead of her sometimes she would say, 'You've got to get behind me; if you get tired, you can lay on the bag and go to sleep.' Sometimes my mother would get a big potato sack, a burlap bag, and she would fix it up so I could hold it up on me to keep warm. I got cold easy enough.

"Later I lived around here in the Bay Area for years until my youngest son and my sister moved to Fresno. When I learned that there was a little grocery store there where I could work, I thought, 'Great, I'll go back home.' But it's not home anymore. Too many killings and too much fighting.

"My last apartment in Fresno had bullet holes just under the window sill. And five bullet holes in our laundry room. I had to keep the lights out and lie there hoping if I didn't make noise, nobody would break in.

"I came back to Mountain View four or five years ago. At first I was with my son and his wife for about eight months. Then one day I got the telephone book out and wrote to all the places around here where there is senior housing with a ceiling on the rent. If I had gone back to Fresno, I would have been living up two steep flights of stairs—like back in the Thirties and Forties. I would never get out of the apartment except to get to the toilet a couple of doors down the hall. But this place where I'm living now called me two days before I was due to go back to Fresno!"

Almira has various health problems that led her to using a scooter: diabetes, osteoporosis, back trouble, and "two or three strokes." She has had surgeries for arthritis in her hips and for low-back disk degeneration.

"I have hardly any feeling now in my legs and my feet. The right leg works pretty darn good, but the other one don't. When they start getting cold, they go to hurting a little bit. I know if I don't warm them up pretty soon, they are going to start to spasm on me.

"The first strokes pulled on the left side, and I can't think to talk sometimes. You should have seen me trying to learn to spell my name again. That was a real doozy, I'm telling you. The strokes left me incontinent, too. The home health nurse comes out from time to time and brings what supplies I need.

"But it's not so bad. I wake up. My aide Rosie comes for me every day. She keeps everything going around here. She vacuums, helps me with my bath, washes clothes, goes to the bank.

"I finally found a doctor that would take Medicare and MediCal, but they don't want to give me any artificial teeth. They wrote the doctor, 'She can't have the artificial teeth. It's not going to cause her death not having the teeth.' Weird people, man.

"My scooter is a Mallard. I was fortunate in getting mine—ten, maybe twelve, years ago—before the company went bankrupt. I wish I could afford a new one, but I don't think Medicare would pay. I'd like to have one with a mechanism to raise and lower the chair. That way I could reach my own cupboards and see what's there. Now I have to either forget it, or take a chance having it all fall on my head!

"I've had this manual wheelchair seven years too, and it has been fixed I don't know how many times. If Medicare don't okay a scooter, all I'll get is another manual wheelchair.

"I like to take the scooter through the fence to the shopping center next door and fool around. One day nobody was there so I was racing the scooter in and out and around. I don't go too far because I've taken to blacking out for no reason. I did it here in the house too and hit my pelvic bone hard enough to fracture it. If I black out while I'm out somewhere, with my luck the scooter would be turned toward the street and I would go right out in traffic."

Almira pointed to her doll collection, visible in the snapshot of her on page 48. "I started collecting dolls about twenty years ago I think. They are all very special in their own way. I love the little doll with the light pink dress and the curls coming down. She just has a real sweet face. She's like a little country girl—dressed up a bit.

51

"I fool around with the dolls, dust them off, and clean the mirrors inside the cabinet. I keep telling everybody I ain't going to order any more. Next thing you know, I've turned around and I'm ordering more!

"I had two more dolls in here but when my year–old grand baby Matthew comes over he thinks they are real babies. One time he wanted to go 'pong!' and he kind of smacked the doll on the leg. His three-year-old brother taught him that! He was trying to get the doll to wake up. I waited to see what he was going to do next. He couldn't get the doll up with that first try so he turned around and hit the doll on the other leg!

"Well, to get back to my apartment, I have a nice place to live and I have a lot of pretty things; I've bought them all myself too. I've got every pleasure conceivable here and beauty is something I admire. So right now, you could say I'm living in the lap of luxury."

IV.

Since My Youth

Alice: "She'll Never Walk Again"

Ann: Living with Arthur

Mayon: Life to Its Fullest

Peggy: No Disability Between the Ears!

Alice Matzdorf

54

Alice Matzdorf

**"In the power chair...I feel I should have a triumphant banner.
You know--excelsior!!!**

It was my good fortune to meet Alice Matzdorf because she was a friend of my brother and sister-in-law. I interviewed her about a year before she died on July 1, 1998 of complications from post-polio syndrome. Several hundred people attended the memorial service for her. Her warmth, energy, humor, and intelligence were bright throughout our interview, as they were for those who spoke of her at the memorial service.

"I grew up in Ossining, north of Tarrytown, New York," she began, "where, at the time, you never *saw* anybody with disabilities. When I was five, I had a very severe case of polio. They thought at first it was the flu or The Grippe. Before it was diagnosed, I was sent to New York city to the Hospital for Joint Diseases. I was in an iron lung for a portion of each day for a couple of weeks. My lungs were not affected, but they weren't sure at first.

"Once they realized that the polio was not going to progress, I was sent home. It was very early in July. I remember my bedroom was upstairs and the window looked over the back yard. We had a lovely back yard. I was watching all the children playing on the swing set and I remember thinking, 'Oh! I'll be out there!' I didn't know what had happened to me. I was able to sit up, but I couldn't move my legs.

"They said at the time, 'Oh, she'll never walk again.' But you can't figure that. I spent two years in rehabilitation. The doctors thought the program at Warm Springs, Georgia would help. Franklin Roosevelt had started the Georgia Warm Springs Foundation and used it for his own polio treatment. By the time I got there, it was quite established. There were cottages for children, adult residences, and a full physical therapy staff. There was a woman in charge of each cottage with maybe fifteen kids. Some children had a parent with them and some didn't.

"It was a ghastly experience for me because I was alone. It was during the Depression. My father was a pharmacist, and we never were hungry or ill-clothed, but money was very scarce. I had an older brother and my mother could not leave the family. My parents thought they were doing the right thing, but they were not psychologically aware.

"People at Warm Springs did not make any attempt to understand children. I was very lonely, and I was not a happy child. I think I must have felt rejected that my parents had sent me away. What did I do to deserve that? I felt really abandoned. But I got through it. While I was there I did a lot of water activities, and I gradually got to the point where I was able to walk for almost all my life, with a cane and a brace. Able in that sense.

"In Warm Springs, I had a life-changing experience. Really an epiphany. I had had surgery in Atlanta, and I was in a body cast—where I spent a lot of my childhood. After surgery they took me back to the infirmary, and on Sundays they would bring our beds onto the patio. What seemed to me at the time a lot of old ladies, probably in their forties, would come to feel sorry for us poor little darlings. They all had, I remember, palmetto fans. It was very hot, and they would stand over us and moan, 'Oooh, oooh, poor little babes,' and they would fan us, and I would want to kill them.

"I remember having these horrible thoughts. But I realized that if I were like that, people wouldn't like me. So I decided to be cheerful. And I made myself cheerful. It happened while I was lying there in bed, as this woman was hovering over me. I can almost remember what she looked like. She said, 'You pooooor...oooh...it must be so terrible...your parents.' and again I thought to myself: I'm either going to scream or smile. It was at that juncture actually that I decided I was going to smile. And I did. And when I came home, I was different. It really did change me. I don't know how it could be explained psychologically, but I couldn't have gotten through that experience if I had not made myself into this more acceptable person.

"In later years, I thought that nobody would ever want to marry me, let alone that I would have children. I never had a date in high school. Never. I was certainly not unattractive, but I had a cane and a brace. There were dances and I had dancing lessons and could dance, but there was never a boy who asked me to go anywhere. Even in college. Of course Vassar at the time was still all women. I think that was actually fortunate because if I had been in a coed situation, it might have been very difficult for me.

"But after college I started seeing young men. They were older and less frightened of the unknown. But there wasn't anyone until I met Kurt in 1950. We were married later that year.

"We had two boys and I didn't want to work when they were young, but at a certain point I was eager to go back to work. I started as the assistant to the vice president for academic affairs at the State University in New Paltz, New York. It was a good job, a very responsible job. I stayed there from January 1970 until June 1994. Kurt and I both officially retired in 1985. But I stayed on part time.

"What happened with the wheelchair was this. Many, many people who have had polio and have reached a certain level of ability, think they're going to stay at that level for the rest of their lives. Decades later however, they suddenly find what doctors think is a recurrence of the polio. It's what they call post–polio syndrome. You get weakness where you never expected it. You just don't function the way you thought you were always going to function. It was a very shocking thing to me. There are now many polio support groups. We started one, although I really don't need it at this point.

"I guess I first began to feel the need for a wheelchair about ten years ago. I was about sixty then. I fought it and fought it. I really didn't want to have to use a wheelchair. I was barely aware of this post–polio syndrome. Finally we bought a manual wheelchair from a wonderful company called Quickie. They were the originators of the lightweight folding wheelchairs. They even make racing wheelchairs—really something!

"I can use crutches but it gets harder and harder. And when I cook, which I love to do, I can only cook standing up. There's something about it...I don't know what it is, habit or whatever. We had the kitchen redone so that it's wheelchair accessible. But I can't cook sitting down. Something up here (pointing to her head).

"For years, we had had an arrangement whereby Kurt would wheel me out to the car, put the chair in the back, and I'd drive off. Wherever I was going, somebody would meet me, take the wheelchair out, and I'd have to be pushed. I *hated* it. Really hated it. I hated (here she whispered) being carried up and down stairs. That to me is the height of indignity. But you know, I did it. All that time I was walking around the house with cane and brace, but I could not go any long distances.

"Then two things happened. I fell and broke my right hip. And," she said somewhat wearily, "I was nearly back to where I had been, when I fell again. This was five years ago. I broke my femur. After that I could not walk with the cane and the brace on my right leg any more.

"When I had polio, it affected my legs, my abdominal muscles, and my back; but my shoulders and my arms had great strength—thank God for that. What I did not know was that there was one muscle in my right shoulder that was affected. With the effects of post–polio syndrome, it began to act up. For many reasons it's annoying; but one of the things I cannot do is propel the manual wheelchair.

"This is where the trusty vehicle I'm using now comes in. We decided it was time to get a power vehicle. I checked into all the three-wheeled vehicles. They are much more 'sportif,' you know, they really are. I would have preferred that. But because I need extra support for my back and even my arms, we felt that I'd be better off with a more supportive thing. This chair I have now is a Quickie too. It's a terrific electric wheelchair.

"To get out of the house, we have a ramp in the front. I take the dog out for a w-a-l-k twice a day. She's asleep so she wouldn't have known I was saying 'walk' anyway. But if she were awake, it would be a different story. My favorite thing is just to *go*. And I meet people for lunch.

"We also bought a Dodge caravan and had it completely converted so that I can use it, supposedly by myself. Also the man who did the van conversion discovered a seat that turns out and then tips down. You place your bottom on the seat and tilt the seat up. It is really a stroke of genius and useful for anybody who has trouble getting into a high van.

"Medicare pays for the wheelchair, but will not modify, or help you modify, a vehicle. With a doctor's letter, you *can* take a medical tax deduction on a van and a swimming pool and a hot tub.

"By the time I get into the front seat of the van, I'm exhausted! So I have been driving much less. And I miss that. Even partially giving it up has been a very difficult thing. That was my real liberation. I used to love to go get lost. If I got upset or depressed, I would get in the car and just drive up to the mountain or somewhere. But you know, that is not really easy any more. The weakness is greater and the discomfort—and this is progressive too.

"But I'm not a depressive person and I've got the freedom of this electric wheelchair, which is really wonderful—in New Paltz or when we travel. We went to Harrisburg for the Bar Mitzvah of one of my great nephews. Kurt and my sister-in-law and I found an Indian restaurant, and it was wonderful because there were curb cuts so that I could get there in the chair. It was a good mile walk, but I got there first!

"We've taken the chair with us to Washington, DC...any place. The wonderful cities are the ones where they have curb cuts. But even when there's not a curb cut, we've found a way. We can tilt the chair back and get the front wheels on the curb. Then I go voom, voom, give it the gas, and get up on the sidewalk. Going down the curb, it's just the reverse.

"I love to go out... even in the middle of winter. I never get cold. The tires on the chair have very good traction. Once the paths are cleared I don't have any problem. I've never gotten stuck. *Ice* I don't like to go out on, but I don't like to *drive* on ice either.

"I have a whole set of funny reactions from people when I'm out in the chair. When I get to the main road, people have said, 'Oh, how do you have the nerve to cross the street?' I say, 'How do *you* have the nerve to cross the street? I'm much faster. I wait for the red light. Isn't that what you do?'

"Then there are people who roll down their car windows and say, 'Hey lady, did you get a ticket yet for speeding? Ha, ha, ha.' But I think it's partially because, when they see a wheelchair with a gray–haired woman in it, they expect to see somebody pushing it; nobody is pushing this and it gives people pause.

"I really love to shock (laughing); I really do. It's part of my nature that's got nothing to do with the polio. My father had the same sense of humor and both our sons do. Their attitudes (about my disability) are wonderful.

"I have good friends in the area too, which really helps a great deal. And some of my college friends come with their husbands about twice a year. They are very dear to me. Considering what I anticipated my life would be like in my down days as an adolescent, and even in my early college years, I have really been so lucky! Lucky in many ways.

"First of all we have been able to afford all these things, which a lot of other people just can't. And I have probably the most wonderful husband in the world. From time to time I think, 'Oh I'm such a burden.' But he doesn't let it be a burden. He's my enabler, he makes certain things easy for me to do, whether I do them or not. I probably would do even less if he were not around. He does things without any flourish, without making me feel he's doing something out of the ordinary. He's a very special person because even when we got married, I had my brace and my cane and was not what you'd call a perfect physical specimen. I think I just expected to go on, single and working, forever. There was no reason for me not to think so. And I thought I'd just age normally.

"Sometimes I feel so childish about what I can do in the chair. From the time I was five, I could never run, I couldn't do a lot of things. Now, in the power chair, all of a sudden I feel I should have a triumphant banner. You know—excelsior!!! Which comes from a poem I knew when I was a kid:

> The shades of night were falling fast
> When through an alpine village pass
> A youth who bore 'midst snow and ice
> A banner with this strange device:
> Excelsior!!!

NB: The lines Alice recalled are from the poem "Excelsior" by Henry Wadsworth Longfellow. In Latin, 'excelsior' means higher or ever upward.

Ann Moore

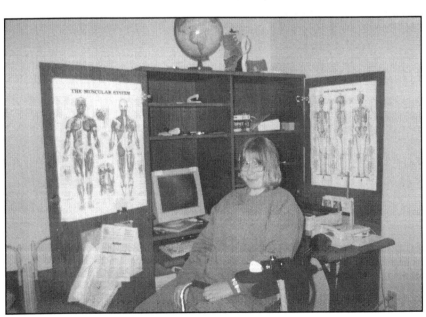

Ann Moore

**"I do have a positive attitude.
I think that's what has gotten me this far!"**

I met Ann scooting around downtown Mountain View. She was thirty-four and had come to California to visit her family while her Dad was working here for a time. Midland, Michigan is their primary home. Ann has had rheumatoid arthritis (RA) since she was young. She needed a total right hip replacement and decided to have the surgery in California where she would have family support.

Ann's disease was not diagnosed until she was nine years old. For a couple of years before that, she had been limping off and on, but nobody identified the problem. While the family was on a vacation in Estes Park, Colorado, she suddenly developed a "swollen knee as big as a bowling ball." She was given some prednisone and the swelling receded, so she continued riding horseback and other vacation activities.

The swelling returned as soon as the prednisone ran its course. When the family returned home, Ann was taken to the Henry Ford Hospital in Detroit, where she was diagnosed with rheumatoid arthritis.

"I'll never forget the shot they gave me at the hospital. The needle looked about this big (stretching her arms apart). I think it took three people to hold me down. They've only given me steroids that one time by injection—then orally for six days twice since then.

"I've never really had pain. I think I've kept it in the back of my mind. If they ever found a cure for this arthritis, I don't think I'd know how to live without it because I've lived with it for so long. I'd probably miss Arthur! (Ann's name for the RA) I sleep with him at night and I wake up with him in the morning. Now I can feel my hip problem. I can't bend over and put on my shoes. When I was younger I could do that."

Ann uses ankle–foot orthotics inside her shoes to stabilize her feet for walking. She has a 'grabber' that she uses to pull a sock onto a form into which she can put her foot; then she pulls out the form and the sock is on her foot—a time–consuming task but a help getting dressed. She finds a cane is very useful: for picking things up from the floor, closing doors, scratching her back, getting mail out of the mailbox, "and killing bugs!"

To get around more easily today, Ann uses an Amigo J9 scooter. She bought it in Michigan where it was manufactured in Bridgeport by the Amigo Company. It has airmatic, radial, all–weather tires, which she says work pretty well in winter. She also has a second scooter, with a hydraulic lift that raises and lowers the chair, which she used when she was working. Health insurance and the local Center for Independent Living helped defray scooter costs.

Ann worked at a hospital in Midland for thirteen years, from 1982 to 1995. She started part time washing pots and pans, then worked in the dish room full time. Finally she got a position where she put silverware, juice, and seasonings on each tray, according to the patient's diet, and carried the trays to the patients.

"The nurses were helping me carry the trays. But it seemed that before my arthritis was acting up, the girls were accepting me like I was. They knew I had rheumatoid arthritis. But when I couldn't walk and I was in the Amigo, they treated me differently.

"They called me names and thought I was being funny. They just made my life harder. I think until a person goes through what we

64

go through, they don't know what it's like. I don't want sympathy for 'poor me,' just to be accepted into everybody's life. If people had been nicer, I think I would have stayed a little longer.

"The Center for Independent Living helped me keep my job as long as I did; I almost lost it because of my disability. I guess what I've learned from working there is that nothing ever stays the same.

"January of '95 was my last month at work. It was just getting too hard. All I could do was work and come home and sleep. I might go back to work there part time after surgery, if everything goes well, or work some place else. I want to do something productive with my life, I like to be around people, and I like computers. My brother Dave gave me a great one."

Ann was getting to work in a 1988 Chevrolet Cavalier. She also used Dial-A-Ride. Here in California she has used Cal Train and she gets to a lot of places in her scooter—downtown, to the parks, around the apartment complex, and in the apartment itself. One time with friends, after getting off a train with the scooter, they had to go through a subway tunnel.

"Our timing was such that we were by ourselves. There were three guys looking at us kind of funny. I think they decided they weren't going to bother us. One man nodded imperceptibly to another, just shook his head 'no.' I could have run them over if they had done something. I thought, 'Next time, I'm going to time it so that other people are there.' I'd like to go over to the Center for Independent Living here in California and see if they offer self-defense classes. Maybe I could do some volunteering too.

"Generally, I'm pretty happy with my life. I can do most of what I want to do, but it takes me longer to do it. It does get really frustrating sometimes, especially when I try so hard not to drop things; it's not worth *trying* not to drop something!

"But I've been reading the Bible quite a bit and that helps my frustration. I just open my Bible and wherever my hand falls, I read that. Bible programs on the radio are good when I'm feeling alone. And it helps to have a supportive family. My parents, two brothers, and a sister all live here in California. And I call my friends; it's kind of nice to have someone your age to talk to.

"One time I decided at the last minute to go on a retreat for people with handicaps. There is a retreat house run by monks at a church in Saginaw, Michigan. It was fun to be with other handicapped people. They weren't all riding an Amigo but a couple of people did.

"Friday night we had a polka band. They finally got me out of the chair and up to dance. That was kind of fun! It was a religious retreat too, where we learned about God and Jesus. And there was time when we were each able to talk about our problems; then you don't feel so bad about yourself. I felt really good after that retreat.

"I go to church whenever I can. I've also been a volunteer receptionist at my church in Midland: answering phones, transferring calls, and taking messages. In Sunday School, I volunteered with third graders who had attention deficit disorders.

"I worked with one girl who was very shy; she sat right next to me. Sometimes she needed help finding the right page. When she thought her answer was right, she'd raise her hand. After I worked with her, she wasn't as shy as she used to be, and she fit in pretty well with the rest of the class. It was fun to watch her progress. I love to work with little children—more than with adults.

"At the church, Mr. Beason helped me get volunteer work. He also helped me bury my dog, a pure-bred Collie, who died of old age. We had to put her to sleep two years ago; but at least I was there with her. I used to take her for a walk with my Amigo; I ran over her feet a couple of times until she got used to it. Friends and family don't want me to get another dog until after the surgery. They are a lot of responsibility, but they sure are a lot of company. Someday I'll get another dog!"

A right hip replacement for Ann took place March 5, 1999 with a Dr. Sherman at Stanford Hospital in Palo Alto, California. In preparation, Ann visited not only the doctor but also several patients who had the same surgery. She found the doctor helped build her confidence and was very understanding. He could see that she was in pain by watching her walk, and that her gait had contributed to the wear and tear on her hip. Other patients' experiences did not help Ann: "They made everything sound so easy." But that was not her experience.

"The days just after surgery are a lot of work; three hours a day with intensive physical therapy. They push you too! Everyone kept telling me the next day was going to be better, and it was. I finally believed them. The doctors say I'll be able to sit on the ground. I haven't been able to do that since I was little.

"Before surgery I couldn't lift the right leg. Now I have full range of motion in my knee and in my hip. The therapists anticipate my using a walker and then walking on crutches for about two months. It will be great to be able to walk again! I'll probably still use the Amigo for long distances.

"Before surgery I was doing a lot of swimming. I get more energy when I go swimming and do isometrics. I hope to be able to bike and get water therapy, water walking at first so I don't dislocate the hip.

"The rheumatologist, a Dr. Singleton, took x-rays of all my bones and said they are in really good condition. My fingers look so pretty on the x-ray: solid white bone. He'll be able to straighten my hands out.

"I guess because I've had osteoarthritis as well as rheumatoid since I was little, I know how to deal with it. Like wearing a pair of shoes, you get used to it. But I think people who don't have a disease can have a hard time too.

"I think this surgery has been really hard on my family. The nurse actually suggested that my Mom go home and get a good night's sleep, that it would be better for both of us. My sister Mary would always talk to me on the phone when I couldn't sleep. My brothers John and David came as much as they could. David brought me some really good 'zines to read and we'd toss a ball back and forth while I was in bed. Dad made sure I did my exercises and that I got a massage. My grandmother Ida and I talked on the phone. Mom was with me all the way through.

"I'm glad I had the surgery done out here, but I'd love to go back home to Michigan—tomorrow if I could!"

Mayon Venerable

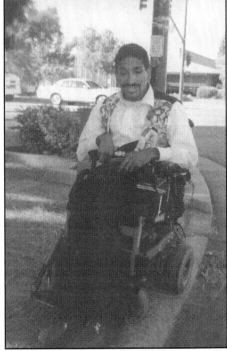

Mayon Venerable

**"My philosophy about life is, You can't give up.
You have to live life to its fullest."**

When I met him, Mayon was waiting at a Mountain View bus stop. He was living with his parents and two sisters, one and seven years younger than he is. An aunt and three younger cousins lived next door.

Mayon was born prematurely in 1978. He has limited use of his hands and uses an electric wheelchair; he cannot walk. One warm May day we sat at a street-side cafe while Mayon told me some of his story.

"I've been living here in Mountain View all my life. To get all the facilities I needed to function, I had to go to school in Palo Alto—starting when I was two years old. I graduated from Gunn High School. It was kind of a drag because all my friends are here in Mountain View.

"But I did what a lot of people don't do now-a-days. I made it through high school. There were a couple of years when I just wanted to drop out and do my own thing. But thanks to my mother's yelling and incessant battling, that wasn't an option for me.

"I grew up hating school because I was never really good at it. I don't think I have any learning disability, I was just slower and it wasn't fun. It's not that I have anything against school, but I had a couple of bad experiences. I had a lot of friends but a lot of people made fun of me, and I just got turned off to the whole school idea. When I graduated, I felt I hadn't learned anything that was practical.

"Right now I am trying to pursue work and a career. Ever since high school, I've worked during the summer with elementary school kids. That's what I like—to work with people. Now I'm looking for office work or work I can do by myself. I need motivation to do something. I don't know if it sounds superficial, but a check coming in every month is motivation enough for me!

"To make some extra money when I was about eleven or twelve, I would go out with my big plastic bag looking for cans to recycle. One day I went out looking for cans as usual. I didn't know my Mom had forgotten to plug in the wheelchair; it has to be charged up every day so it doesn't run out of energy. I got stuck on a speed bump in the middle of a road. The chair ran out of juice and I couldn't move.

"No cars came for about twenty minutes and I wasn't going to sit there like a potato waiting for someone. So I got out of my chair. At that point I was as low as the street. No one would be able to see my body, so they could have crushed me like a melon. I tried to push my wheelchair over the speed bump, but it was too heavy. So I decided to crawl to the sidewalk and hope my chair didn't get stolen. I was on my way when I hit some broken glass and cut my arm.

"My arm was all scraped up and cars were coming. My head was about to be crushed like a melon, but some guy I didn't even know darted out into the street, scooped me up, put me back in my wheelchair, and pushed me to where my Mom was working.

"For a long time I would tell my story and the only one who would believe me was my Mom because she saw all the cuts and scrapes on my arms. It was pretty amazing that I even survived. And my chair could have been stolen.

"I have also had some major surgeries. When I was two years old, I had my eyes worked on because they were crossed. And I broke my hip in a hockey accident. I was in eighth grade, playing gym hockey. All these people in wheelchairs went after the puck. A girl side-swiped me and my hip snapped. Then when I was in high school, I was speeding down this ramp, not watching where I was going, and I crashed full speed with my shins into a steel table. I smashed it so hard, my ankle snapped in two. I had to go to the doctor.

"Fifty or sixty percent of my trips to the hospital are because of what I did to myself. Because I'm kind of reckless. But, I wouldn't have it any other way. I would rather live life like I am doing right now than live life slower and slower all the time.

"I know a lot of people who are sheltered and don't get to experience life. I really thank my Mom and my Dad because they have been there to teach me to be independent. The first time that I was independent in my motorized wheelchair was at the age of five. At first, it was a disaster. I crashed into walls. I was so young and the chair wasn't as sophisticated as this one—but it got me around.

"I've had this Quicky P 300 since I was ten years old and about five inches shorter. I did have foot supports, but once I bashed into a curb so hard that one of the metal footrests broke in half. I'm not paralyzed and I can feel everything.

"I wear out wheelchairs the way people wear out shoes. Right now my tires are kind of messed up because, to be frank, I'm not real careful with my driving. I've outgrown this wheelchair, but I'm in the process of getting a new one—through Rehab Specialists in Mountain View.

"Most of the people I've met keep their wheelchairs on slow speed so they don't go too fast. But as you see—this wasn't on purpose—I broke off the speedometer, and it was on high speed so now I'm stuck there. To go slowly I don't push the control all the way. If I did that here, I'd push the table here in the restaurant off the curb!

"I have had it plenty hard. I grew up too early. I was never care-free as a child, so now I just want to do what I want. With everything I do, I have to give two-hundred percent just to do what other people do. Have you ever tried crawling up stairs while other people

71

can just run up the stairs? I have to take five minutes to crawl up. But still, I manage to do it!

"For a long time I was so angry inside; to a point I still am. I'm just beginning to be able to control it. Bad tempers and bullheadedness run through my family. If I get in a bad mood I just go off at people. It's not right, but that's part of who I am. And so for each friend, I have an equal number of enemies.

"When I get angry I'm a danger to myself and to others. It doesn't frighten me; it frightens other people. But, I've been able to contain it and work through a lot of that anger. I still have some regrets, and I still wake up sometimes wondering, 'Why was I chosen to go through this hell?'

"In no way am I very religious. I do believe in God and I should go to church more often. I skip out of church even at Christmas and Easter, which isn't·right. My Mom pushed me to do a lot of good things, but every time I go to church, the priests feel sorry for me.

"There's a place in the holy communion ceremony where you have to go up to the priest and confess your sins. One time I went up and I was scared because at the time I had gotten into a tremendous fight in the school bathroom with a guy who made fun of me. My upper body is really strong so I was able to beat the guy, and then I spat on him.

"So I was all ready to tell the priest, when he looked down and blessed me; he didn't hear a word I was saying. He felt so sorry for me—when I had hurt someone real bad. I don't want people to feel sorry for me. I want people to like me for who I am. In that church I don't get that.

"There have been a couple of times I just said, 'Why? Why did this have to happen to me?' And there have been a couple times I said, 'Why bother?' I have to thank my parents again because they were there for me, to pull me out of it.

"And my sisters and all three cousins were there for me when I was having a hard time with my Mom. We grew up and spent a lot of time together so we have this special bond. They've always been like friends to me and I really appreciate that. Every time I've been in a slump, they have been there to pull me out of it too.

"But my philosophy about life is, You can't give up. You have to live life to its fullest. You can't slow down. You can't be scared of what might happen. I don't want to have to say I missed out on doing something. I'm not going to slow down until I'm old and ready to die.

"I envision marriage and family, but not until way later. It's strange because I have never in my whole life envisioned having a wife who is in a wheelchair like me. A lot of people I've run into in wheelchairs do.

"If I have kids, I only want to have one. Kids are a big responsibility and with all the stuff I've been through, I don't think I would be able to handle more than one.

"Right now I'm in a pretty good place. We've just moved and I'm not as angry as I used to be. I've been able to express myself in other ways. I did some drawing and whenever I found myself getting angry, I read a book or did something like that. The basic thing for me is to just walk away. Especially with my Mom. I love my Mom to death, but we have had our share of discussions, as we call it. Sometimes I just 'walk' away so I don't get too explosive inside.

"My Mom has been trying to get me into a support group. I don't do support groups very well. Either I'm closed off or I talk a lot of B.S. I'd rather just flock to wherever all my friends are and talk to people on the street. I hang out with able–bodied people.

"If I started hanging out with disabled people, I would be a hypocrite. I fought so hard to get able–bodied friends that going into a support group would be a step down. For my mental health, I would be much better off going to a one–on–one counseling session. I don't like a lot of people opening my business.

"Trust me! Sometimes I'm the most unappreciative person you can ever imagine. Especially to my mother. I've fought with my Mom and I've threatened to move out; but I'm going to look back when I'm twenty–six or so and say, 'Where has all those arguments with my Mom gotten me?' Some day my Mom's going to be dead, and then I'm going to be sorry.

"But I still get up every morning. I'm a pretty happy, easygoing, outgoing guy. For a long time I couldn't ignore the snickers and all the bad looks I got—which contributed to some more anger. But over the years I've been able to grow and work through that. I did it for me because it was tearing me up inside. And if my family hadn't been there for me I probably would have died. Just from my mental anguish.

"In finishing, I would just like to give a shout out to my family and all of my friends and everyone who has been there to support me and treat me like everyone else. I thank them a lot. And thank you for giving me the chance to tell you about my life."

A few months ago, I saw Mayon tooling along the street in his wheelchair. He was wearing the kind of vest that employees at the Century movie houses wear. He told me that he had a job there and that he had moved out and was living on his own. I sometimes see him at the theater working. He is now going to college as well!

Peggy Webber

Peggy Webber

"People thought that if you had a visible disability, there was also a disability in the space between your ears."

Peggy Webber lives in San Jose, California near the City College campus from which she graduated. She shares her home with an attendant, her dog, cats, and a rabbit. A friend of mine who saw her wheeling along the street introduced me to her. Later we met and talked in her home.

"I contracted polio when I was eight and have been in a wheelchair since then because I can't walk. We lived in Kansas, and Kansas had no plans in the 1940s to educate the disabled. Nothing. Eventually a lady who happened to come by collecting for the March of Dimes let it slip that she was a substitute teacher. My mother basically kidnapped her and threw her into my room with, 'Peggy, she's a teacher!' People thought that if you had a visible disability, there was also a disability in the space between your ears.

"As soon as she saw that there was nothing wrong with my mind, she arranged to have me registered with the school district. She was going to the homes of students who had a short–term illness—like really bad asthma or a broken leg or arm. I was the first one who was just disabled.

"My Dad was in the service and after World War II, we were transferred to Japan. The school there was run by the military, and they didn't have anything in their books about having to be able-bodied to go to school. So my mother, and later other school friends, took me to school in my wheelchair on a daily basis.

"I've always had a job of one sort or another, and I had my first job there in Japan when I was fourteen. I was secretary to the Catholic chaplain on the military base in Tokyo. It worked into almost forty hours a week. I wasn't making secretary wages, but thirty-five to forty bucks a months seemed like a lot of money then.

"In 1955 we were sent to California. Here you were required to attend school until you were at least sixteen, so they had home teachers set up. Those of us who were disabled could take advantage of it. I received my high school diploma from San Francisco Unified High School District. Then when we came to Santa Clara County, I attended City College and received an AA degree.

"My folks didn't raise me to think that I was going to be dependent on someone every day of my life, but with the thought that I would eventually be independent and on my own.

"I've done television market research since April of 1963: political surveys, financial studies, market studies, interviews of people for radio, and television rating studies. I have used the computer for marketing work for a charitable organization. So having the computer has been a necessary means. I play games on it too. All them shoot 'em up, bang 'em ups!

"For a long time I was using only a manual wheelchair, and to get out of the house, I had to depend on the friendliness of other people. It becomes very hard to continually ask the same people to help you go shopping, and then have to tell them to get lost so you can buy for them as well! Always being dependent on somebody else to get out is for the birds. I absolutely can't stand that kind of a routine.

"Since 1991 I have had a power wheelchair to use at home. I also have this Palmer, a big electric four-wheeler: to go to the malls, to a wedding, to meet people. I've been to nearby towns: Sunnyvale,

Cupertino, and into Santa Clara. I have a hoist in the garage where—by myself—I can get from the wheelchair to the Palmer and back.

"My Palmer is a big one. It's like a golf cart if you take a real look at it, with two batteries, and it goes about ten to twelve miles an hour on the straightaway. You can go about thirty or forty miles on a charge. There's much less possibility of tipping over in the Palmer than on a three-wheeler, which I couldn't handle at all because I couldn't stand up or even crawl back into it. I tried smaller ones and they felt so unsteady I was afraid to even move. So I got the Palmer and I feel much more secure.

"With the basket in the back I go grocery shopping in it. I brought home a three-piece stereo system all at one time! I brought home a color television and a microwave. It also brings home the cat and dog and rabbit food. I go down to the feed and grain store and get 100 or 150 pounds of food at a time, and I can bring it home in that basket. I didn't bring home the computer. I made the store bring it home. You don't want to bang that. The Palmer doesn't have the kind of shock absorbers a car has. But having the Palmer gives me so much more independence.

"Of course, I broke my foot in it once too. That was one of the times when the silly spring on the accelerator broke. I had been grocery shopping and when I got to the cash register I had a load of groceries so I turned the Palmer off. I thought I heard a ping but you hear a lot of things in a grocery store. The groceries were run through. I paid the bill. They had everything in the sacks, in the basket, tied down with the bungy cord. I turned on the motor and because that spring had broken, the accelerator rolled right up, and I left that store at thirteen miles an hour!

"The doors didn't have a chance to open all the way, but they've got a quick breakaway if they're hit hard. So they broke away—flew up in the air and dropped down behind me. I was already out, but there was a motor home parked across the wheelchair ramp. And I broadsided it. It threw me forward and I broke my foot!

"That shows you what can happen at thirteen miles an hour! What would happen if you were going twenty-five miles an hour? Well, I was in that Palmer, and there was enough between me and the motor home to protect me. I tore off the arm of the Palmer and one of the turn signals. The motor home, which was illegally parked, left before anybody got there.

"The store manager called 911 and reported that a lady in a wheelchair had gone through their front door. They sent two police officers who knew CPR, a fire truck with paramedics, and the super duper ambulance that can almost do surgery on board. And because there was a doctor standing there when this call came through, he figured I was going to be a bloody, almost-dead mess and he had jumped on board. And they were looking for the victim!

"They asked the lady behind me—I guess she was the one who looked the most pale—if she were the victim. She shook her head no and pointed at me! I said, "Well, I think all I did was sprain my ankle." It turned out it was broken. But I had all this help! They thought if I went through the door, that meant broken glass. So they were expecting to find me out flat on the pavement with jagged chunks of glass. They were not expecting to see me sitting upright.

"I went home then because I thought all I had was a sprain. A couple of hours later, the ankle had swelled to the size of a beach ball and it was throbbing. I called Medicare and they took me to O'Connor Hospital emergency. When we got there the nurse said, "Is this the lady who broadsided the motor home?" The guy who was pushing me on the stretcher was cracking up. The nurse was grinning. And the rest of the patients in the waiting area were staring at me wondering why I didn't look damaged! And probably wondering, how did I broadside the motor home? What was I driving? They had no idea that I was driving a wheelchair.

"I've also had a couple of strokes. The first stroke happened after I had an allergic reaction to penicillin May seventeenth of '94. When I woke up I was in ICU sucking a respirator. My right lung had collapsed, and there was a tube up my nose and into my stomach, and one in my chest. I was on a urinary catheter and had two IVs going at all times. Plus I was on a bed that breathes—inflates and deflates to prevent bedsores. They had wrappings on my legs that did the same thing—they breathed too.

"So, given those circumstances I felt a little strange. This stroke was no doubt brought about by everything else that was going sideways. But it was hard to tell that I'd had a stroke until I had been home a while.

"The first day on my own was a week after I got home from the hospital. Friends were gone and my attendant was away for the day. I fixed myself a mug of soup and carried it back to my room on my left leg. It felt a little warm, but when I finished the soup, the skirt was sticking to me. I had a blister on my leg about three inches long, half an inch wide, and raised up about half an inch. I hadn't felt a thing. It was then that I knew I'd had a stroke!

"The only time I was really stopped was the day the chair died and I had a second stroke—December 23, 1994. We didn't realize my big Palmer wasn't charging, and I ran out of juice at six o'clock in the evening while I was shopping. I had just finished getting things for Christmas—including going to Andy's Pet Shop to pick up a lovebird for a girlfriend who was upholstering a chair for me.

"I had the bird in my basket on the Palmer—having just suffered a stroke which I hadn't bothered to tell anybody had happened. The left side of my body was totally numb at that point. Fortunately there was a man in a pickup truck in the parking lot reading his Bible. He got out of the truck and pushed me the half mile home into my garage. Somehow I got out of the chair and into the house.

"When I had been home about half an hour, my girlfriend noticed the left side of my face was drooping. I told her I had had a stroke a few hours back. And she about had a cow, 'You're going to the doctor!' I said, 'No I'm not. I've got an appointment on the 28th of December.' She was certain I was out of my mind. Well, it didn't kill me, but I was down to about half the muscle strength I had had in that arm. Now, it's built back up.

"Last Christmas was another time my attendant had some time off. We had all but one day covered and my eighty-year-old mother said she could do it! My brothers would have a fit, I thought, so we didn't tell them until after the fact. But she got me in and out of bed and did everything that I can't do for myself. Good ol' stubborn Irish stock!

"Most of my other friends are people I have met through marketing or when I'm out in the Palmer. I know some of my mother's friends now as well. I try to know her neighbors so that if something were to happen to her, they would be able to get hold of me.

"Last but not least, I also know people through the Catholic church here in San Jose. I go down there part of the time, and once a month they come to the house to bring communion. If it isn't one of the priests, one of the sisters comes. Sister Rosemary in particular. Because where she lives they don't want pets. She gets her pet fix when she comes here!"

V.

Couples

Jaclin and Paul Burtzlaff

Jaclin: "The scooter has kept me functioning like a human being...
and sometimes I forget that I have a handicap, and then all of a
sudden, I'm stuck out in the middle of somewhere and not able to
negotiate easily. But when I dream, I don't have any handicap.
In dreams I'm perfect. (laughter) Why not!"

Paul: "People seem to think that you have to be in your death
bed before you use a scooter... But... it is just a means of getting
around for people who can't walk well...
When you become disabled,
you learn a lot of things, all kinds of little tricks
that you pick up as you go along."

The interview with Jaclin and Paul Burtzlaff took place at a
Sunnyvale, California coffee shop. Their relationship felt like the
heart of the interview, which is presented as a conversation. This is
followed by a separate, nuts and bolts discussion with them about
scooters: types, access, lifts and hitches, and repair.

Jaclin: We got introduced to the whole scooter business because my local Safeway had scooters (for shoppers to use in the store) just about the time I became handicapped (with hardening of the arteries). It was wonderfully, wonderfully liberating for me! Finally I could go grocery shopping, get on the scooter, and start scooting around.

Paul: The model we have now is a Forster 2000. A three-wheeler with six-inch wheels. We share the scooter. We live in a mobile home park and we both walk, so we just switch places from walking to scootering. That way we can travel all over the country, and we always have the opportunity to get exercise. Everyone asked, "What do you need a scooter for?"

Jaclin: We're not sixty-five yet.

Paul: I want it; I don't need it. People seem to think that you have to be in your death bed before you use a scooter. Or they think of it like a wheelchair, that you are totally disabled. But it isn't true. It is just a means of getting around for people who can't walk well for one reason or the other—because of age or weight or something. (Paul is a smoker and has difficult-to-diagnose stomach pain.) At least they can get out and go somewhere.

Paul moved to California from Chicago in 1965; Jaclin came in 1971. They met in 1977.

Jaclin: I was forty-three years old and had just concluded that God, or the universe, or fate, had decided that I wasn't going to be married. I had been married young and divorced for twenty years when I met Paul. I broke a little chip off the end of the bell curve by meeting a life partner twenty years later when they say your chances of marriage are less than zero.

Jaclin's Health
Jaclin: Back to more recent history. I became ill the summer of '94. I had had symptoms—couldn't walk as far as I used to, couldn't run. My doctor used the word claudication. I didn't associate that with general hardening of the arteries until they finally told me I had to have a heart bypass as well as surgery to allow blood to flow in my right leg. I was out of circulation for five months.

It was only when I was in the hospital for my first surgery in 1994 that I ever got it that there was healthful eating. I feel that if I had had proper information earlier on, for example limiting fat in the diet, things might have been different.

It wasn't until Thanksgiving that I was finally discharged and went back to work. I could walk at that point with a cane well enough to get around the office, but I sure wasn't doing anything much.

The following summer ('95), I had to have surgery in my other, left, leg. I thought that I had done everything needed to reverse the hardening of the arteries, but it wasn't true. So that was an additional setback. Then, during the summer of '96 I had to go in for a retread on that left leg because the vessel the doctor had used the first time effectively collapsed. So right now, I am just working on staying alive for the next ten years.

The scooter has kept me functioning like a human being, like a housekeeper. If I had to stay on my feet without the scooter, I would have to depend on Paul to grocery shop for me. Which is a totally different experience. It wouldn't be an experience; I'd be housebound.

In the house, I'm never far from a wall or a piece of furniture. I've tripped quite a bit because since the first leg surgery, I've lost the anterior compartment muscles in my lower leg. I can't raise the front of my right foot—called foot drop—so my gait is all uneven. If I had it on both sides I wouldn't have a problem. (laughter) The doctors didn't think I would be able to walk effectively or drive again.

The foot drop is a pain in the neck, but it's a very minor thing. I can walk! When there's pain, I sit down and wait until I can get up and walk again.

I'm getting stronger all the time. At one time I could walk only a few feet. Then I could walk a few minutes. Now, on my treadmill I can go half a mile without stopping—in relative comfort. Out of doors it would take more time to go the same distance. The circulation is improving, and I have a pair of orthopedic shoes being made by Davis Shoe Therapeutics in San Francisco. I expect they will lift the drop foot.

Paul's Health

Jaclin: My surgery was for hardening of the arteries. Paul's was because of smoking; he doesn't have a problem with fat in his bloodstream. Paul has been in pain recently, and he's not a man who yields to pain.

Paul: The last doctor said, "We don't know what's wrong with you. You're a mystery;" and that was it. They were going to just let me live out the rest of my life this way.

I never know if I'm hungry or not. My stomach always feels full. When I walk, I lean forward because my stomach hurts. It's bulged out. They thought it was some blockage. So I did the scan and the barium enema. Had to take milk of magnesia or whatever it was. Gallons. (laughter)

Jaclin: Eating chalk for a colonoscopy.

Paul: They can't find any blockage. I accused the surgeon of cutting off the tip of his rubber glove and leaving it in there. So that every time I breathe, my stomach blows up like a balloon. He took me seriously too. I was joking.

Jaclin: I don't know when Paul's joking. He teases me all the time. He's trying not to smile. So I take everything he says seriously.

Paul: The pain is getting worse. I can't walk. I can hardly even ride the scooter. They're talking about doing an MRI—standing up. So now I've got to design a jack so they can tip one of those MRI magnets on its end.

Jaclin: Somewhere in the Bay Area there is a standing MRI— we've both heard about it. The MRI will show what's happening.

Paul: I don't know how long they would have let us go on if I hadn't called the doctor and said, "Wait, wait, wait; this is not working." Other people would have waited, I guess. You have to fight for what you want.

In health care generally, two things are happening simultaneously. All the costs are going up. I know the difference between what they used to pay me as a respiratory therapist and what they are paying the kids who are going into it now. And all that sophisticated equipment is expensive. They've got to make a profit and charge for the research too. Also the population is aging—in part because antibiotics have increased our lifespan. As for my own situation, several years ago I had three surgeries. Six weeks apart.

Jaclin: He had two carotid endartectomies and an aorto-femoral bypass (see the Glossary for definitions) to improve the circulation in his neck and groin. Then he was home, and I was home, and the most important thing in my life has been exercise.

Paul had been using the bicycle for months, maybe even years. So he had been getting regular exercise. But right after the surgery he couldn't lift his legs up and down the stairs.

So we got the scooter. The first thing we used it for was to go out in the evening. I would start walking, and when I gave up, I would take the scooter. Then when he got to the point where he couldn't take another step, I would walk a little more, and so forth. It worked beautifully.

The Honeymoon

Jaclin: Then I was thinking we had never really had a honeymoon, only a trip together to New Orleans many years ago. I saw an advertisement for a Disneyland celebration. And I said to Paul, "Why don't we go?"

We finally got it all together and took a month's vacation in Southern California: to Disneyland, Seaworld, the Wild Animal Park in San Diego. The scooter was very effective in all of those places. In most of them they have special entrances for people who are handicapped, which worked very well. AAA gave us a Free Parking pass and a break for a three-day ticket to Disneyland. So we made use of those, and we had disabled placards of course for parking.

I had warned Paul before the trip, "O.K. you are retired, nobody's keeping score, we don't have to be anywhere any time. Sometimes the facilities don't have a lot of redundancy. We might have to plan in advance. And if plans don't work out, we might have to wait a long time." I was trying to prime him for this so that when the first thing came up that didn't happen just as we wanted, the whole thing wouldn't be ruined for him. It's a new mind-set.

When we got to Los Angeles, we found that the ticket for something wasn't right, and we had to wait twenty-four hours. Well, what do you know, we found something else on our list that was wonderful and exciting to do. We have both learned that's just part of traveling—anywhere.

Paul: It's interesting. When you become disabled, you learn a lot of things, all kinds of little tricks that you pick up as you go along. We used the scooter when we went out to theater restaurants. We were able to get more space at the table.

Jaclin: So you've got more elbow room. (laughter)

Paul: There are a lot of things disabled people don't understand. They may think they are more limited than they really are. And many people who are not disabled assume maybe you are in trouble even if you aren't, and they'll ask if they can help you across streets, or they direct traffic. People are pretty good that way.

Jaclin: I'm terrible in that respect because whenever I need to be finding trouble, I want to do it myself! (Jaclin has a taste for adventure!)

Paul: We even took our scooter on a ship—from Los Angeles to Ensenada. We stopped at San Diego and Catalina Island. I couldn't take the scooter off the ship at Catalina because there was no dock; they got us out in little boats. When you get to the island you can rent golf carts. In San Diego I wanted to get off the ship but the entrance was blocked. So the ship's crew just lifted the scooter, carried it down the steps, and got me off the ship that way.

And I went on the light-rail in Ensenada. You sit on a lift, the operator raises you up, and you wheel right on. In Tijuana they charged two dollars on a special bus for the handicapped. They got me to wherever I wanted to be dropped off.

For real adventure, next time I'm in L.A. I'll take the scooter up the escalator—you can't see if it has steps; which it doesn't—and I'll take a picture. (laughter) That's the first time I got scared on that scooter. When I first got all three wheels on that escalator belt, it started to tip over backwards. I had to grab the rails to keep it upright. All the weight is toward the back. All of a sudden, I was going over backwards. I don't scare easy but...

At the San Diego Zoo, the scooter broke down and we got lost. It was a big day. There were fifty thousand people there.

Jaclin: A special day.

Paul: We got lost within ten feet of each other. For a couple of hours we couldn't find each other. I was going to purchase a couple of walkie talkies before we went on the trip, but I hadn't.

Jaclin: I couldn't find that man to save my life. I must have been looking right at him; I was looking for his white hair.

Paul was on the scooter and I didn't have a place to sit down. I had just had surgery in June and it wasn't easy. But I was able to walk because there was always a fence or railing.

I got myself to the security office, but they were so swamped they weren't taking messages. So I figured Paul would end up where the lost children are—I was a lost kid. I found a plain old ordinary wooden chair, sat there and waited, and sure enough... But it was about an hour and a half later. Paul said the scooter's clutch had burned out.

Paul: It overheated and I could smell it, so I just stopped. Security asked if I could ride it downhill to a place where they could bring a van. Once I started downhill, I couldn't stop because I had no brakes. So I rode it downhill about forty miles an hour. I have a hand brake but my tires are notched like snow tires, so you can't use that hand brake. If it catches in one of those notches...

Jaclin: It'll throw you. It will stop, and then you go forward. And I wouldn't advise anybody to do that.

Paul: When I got to the bottom it was pretty flat, so I just went around in circles about eight times. Finally it stopped. Security got us back together and they brought a van and about three people lifted the scooter into the van, and unloaded it into our car out in the parking lot. That was our zoo adventure.

At Disneyland, they gave us a special handicap map and directions for getting in and out of rides. You always go into an exit, so you don't stand in line. Then when you get off the ride, the scooter is there waiting for you. We were able, in five days, to see every show. Most people can't because you waste all your time standing in lines.

Jaclin: And people are curious. Paul got a horn for me—a little yellow horn—and put it on the handlebars so I could let people know that I was in back of them; and this attracted much attention!

When we were at Disneyland every single employee wanted to toot our horn. Kids wanted to come over and toot the horn. It's interesting that you see a horn and you just want to toot it.

Paul also bought us safety vests made of raincoat material. They're pretty bright. We also brought back some flags that we'll put on someday.

Paul: At the Hotel del Coronado in San Diego, I didn't want to pay five dollars an hour for parking for lunch so we parked two blocks away. We couldn't walk far, but we had the scooter.

Jaclin: We even took the scooter into the dining room. All the way to our table! Because we are seniors we have AARP and we got a lot of discounts. One little part of our adventure was finding all the coupons and discounts and taking advantage of them.

Paul: It's amazing what you can do with coupons. You can travel pretty reasonably. And, you're treated well.

Jaclin: It's been quite an adventure. Quite an adventure. I credit Paul one-hundred percent.

It's very nice in our case; I have a partner. If you are alone it's a different story. It's very important to have a buddy and a nurturing buddy; you can have a life partner who *doesn't* function that way too. But, when two of you are working on it, if you can just keep your cool, your calm, there must have been only one or two places that we couldn't go or didn't go.

We are not terribly handicapped. When we have had to get up and walk on our own two legs, we've been able to do it. I can even go up and down stairs without a banister if Paul walks in front of me and I put my hand on his shoulder. With a banister I'm fine alone. And I take my cane with me where ever I go.

In real life, sometimes I forget that I have a handicap, and then all of a sudden, I'm stuck out in the middle of somewhere and not able to negotiate easily. But when I dream, I don't have any handicap. In dreams I'm perfect. (laughter) Why not!

Moving

Paul: We're moving to the Carmel and Monterey area in a few months. We'll be on the beach a lot with the scooter. We're going to die on the beach. We'll be beach bums for the rest of our lives. I can get a scooter with four-wheel drive and bigger tires and ride the sand all day long. We'll probably wind up with two scooters again.

Jaclin: Oh, come on...I'm going to wind up on two feet! But walking on the sand is difficult anyway. Two scooters will be fun.

Paul: They've got plugs all over the place where you can charge the batteries, so you can go for days if you want to. I have been a mechanical engineer, so I know most of this stuff about scooters. My motor is a little heavier than most. I've got one point one (1.1) horsepower so you can do things like go across grass. We wound up going through sand in Balboa Park in San Diego. I just drove right through it.

I can take the scooter indoors now, but I won't be able to when we get into a new house. Because we're going to have white carpeting! Don't use the scooter inside and outside if you've got white carpeting! Unless you like (the tweed effect of) Berber. Instant Berber!

More About Scooters

Before buying a scooter, some things to consider are scooter styles, access, lifts, hitches, and repairs. The discussion that follows highlights the Burtzlaffs' experience with these practicalities.

Jaclin: "I think all this is important because we are looking at a population that's aging, and has more leisure, and wants to do trips. And what do you do when you are on a trip? You walk!"

Scooters

Paul: I'm learning more and more about the people who need scooters. The prices are going up so high, a lot of people who need them can't afford them. And Medicare won't pay for certain models.

An organization for the handicapped called New Ability has a big show every year, in different places around the country. Wheelchairs are part of it. It was in San Mateo the year I went. There were some new requirements. Apparently Medicare will not pay for a four–wheel scooter. I guess that encourages you to use it outside—not just inside. And they might think you really don't need it.

In response, a company has come out with the Rascal. You buy the three-wheel scooter and Medicare pays for it. Then you can buy a two-wheel front tiller separately and just clamp it on. Anyone can handle the quick release, disconnect the single wheel, and put on the two-wheel tiller. So you have four wheels, which are safer and more stable than three. Then you travel around the world!

There are also scooters built for two people—side by side. And they have them with twelve-inch, fourteen-inch, and even bicycle wheels. They look like a golf cart.

On the double-seat scooter, the seat is fixed. On a single scooter, make sure the seat swivels. I think most of them do now. If you come to a dinner table on the scooter, you want to swivel ninety degrees so you can face the table to eat.

Several other manufacturers also came out with a unit that looks almost like the electric wheelchair. It's got twenty-inch wheels instead of six-inch wheels.

It doesn't have the steering tiller; it's a hand control like a wheelchair—and it turns on a dime. It also carries a bigger battery so you can go farther and faster. You can even climb as much as fifteen degree inclines with it. So people are buying that now. And it qualifies one-hundred percent for Medicare or other insurance.

For outdoor use you really want four wheels on the ground instead of three. And manufacturers are putting in springs and shock absorbers so when the way is uneven, the scooter will level itself out. Just like a car.

The new scooters have built-in chargers or little portables that you can fit in your coat pocket and plug into any outlet. Just in case you run out of juice. I did run out of juice when I used to own boats. I would gas up and keep going, and forget that I had to come back. There were no gas stations in the middle of the delta or the lake. Now even at Disneyland, you know, they've got outlets outside near the parking lot. And the newer chargers have two speeds—both a faster and a slower charge.

In England they have higher-powered scooters, and they are shipping them into the United States now. The requirements in England are the same as for a car here, or a golf-cart used on the street. They don't have curb cuts yet, so you have to ride in the street there.

Insurance companies will cover damage. But they will not insure the scooter for theft on the back-end of a car or in a van. So you have to make sure that you have a chain on it.

Jaclin: We also changed from a key to a switch so that somebody couldn't just take a hairpin, turn it on, and go away with it. But Paul was telling me the scooter is not something that you can get money for. It's not an easily fenced product.

Paul: Manufacturers are looking more toward the handicapped generally, not only those who can't use their legs. They are putting wheels on scooters that are as much as fourteen inches in diameter, twice the size of mine. They are making them more compact and the batteries are getting larger so you can get more miles—as much as forty miles on some. Just make sure you only go twenty miles so you can get back! They are also coming out with front-wheel and rear-wheel drives so you can climb hills. You can use it in San Francisco as a four-wheel drive.

Access

Paul: The disabilities act wasn't passed until 1990. Places that were built twenty-five, thirty years ago, can't accommodate easily for wheelchair accessibility. Disneyland has twenty-six-inch-wide escalators to get to the monorail. If you have a twenty-eight-inch wheelchair or scooter you can't get onto the walking escalator to the monorail. I just got on it; I had one inch on each side. They don't have steps; you get onto it, and then it levels out. At the other end we could take the elevator, go downstairs, and eat at the restaurant.

Make sure that the scooter isn't over twenty-four inches wide. Hubcap to hubcap. That's the widest you can go on the rides too. You can't even maneuver inside any older house with a three-wheeler if you are over twenty-four inches wide.

Some motels have handicap areas like the third floor of the hotel in Disneyland. You get onto the elevator and you can drive into the rooms, even the smallest.

Jaclin: Sometimes it's not the doorway itself, but the fact that the door overlaps into the doorway, and you can't completely open the door.

Paul: When you purchase a scooter, get a v–shaped, door–opening bumper on the front. Not all shopping malls have electric doors. You can always get out of a shopping mall because all exit doors have to open out; and you push the door out. But, you can't get yourself in. So you've got to wait for somebody to open the door.

Jaclin: That happens in the bathrooms too. I can remember letting him into bathrooms and having to wait for someone to let him out. (chuckling)

Lifts and Hitches

Paul: Lift stations are made to put on the back end of the car, but you have to have a big car. The newer cars are not able to carry these scooters easily. I had to manufacture my own trailer hitch and method of mounting so I could carry one scooter. I couldn't carry two.

Some of the smaller scooters are light enough to break down into three pieces and put into the trunk. You have to have some strength (or help from others) to lift a fifty-pound motor into the trunk; most trunks are too high, though I can get mine up onto the bumper of my car and just slide it in.

If you want to carry more than one scooter, you need a van, but our one scooter rides outside on the trailer. I drive it on; its electric elevator lifts it up; then you clamp it down. It only takes two minutes. The first day, I did have problems with people wanting to know what's holding the scooter. The trailer's invisible!

The scooter's high enough so you can't see out the back window. I decided to put a loud back–up alarm on it. As well as a tail light, stop light, and back–up light—so everybody sees me and hears me.

Repairs

Paul: I did find something very interesting in San Diego. You don't have to go to a particular manufacturer; you can go to anybody who repairs scooters. I thumbed through the yellow pages to get my scooter repaired, and I wound up with a pharmacy that does repairs. And they were able to loan us a scooter while they repaired ours.

Jaclin: This man at the San Diego pharmacy knew exactly what the trouble was. I had burned out a clutch and the brake. We just had to wait three days for the part to be FedEx'ed from wherever it came from.

Paul: The clutch releases and expands away from the brake. So, when it's being used, like going downhill or uphill, and you get a little bit of friction between your clutch and the brake, it actually charges your battery. It acts as a generator. But mine locked up.

In the meantime, I started shopping for a four–wheel drive. Apparently the drug companies buy them in bulk. And these pharmacies sell them to their customers. But you can't buy accessories, just the basic scooter.

Tom and Joan
Nance

Joan and Tom Nance

Joan: "If you cannot walk, the (three-wheeled) scooter's not the thing for you. Sometimes you have to put your foot out to catch yourself... with three wheels you can tip very easily on the curbs. If a person cannot walk, they should have four wheels."

Tom: "I went to Korea as a young man and I sometimes wonder how I came out of there... One day I started talking about it. I've had very few...nightmares since. I'm convinced that that's the secret... So I sat down and wrote."

Joan and Tom moved to Mountain View about a year before I met Joan riding on her scooter. They now lived in a place that required less outside work than their Redwood City home of 26 years. The three of us talked later at their apartment, about scooters and about life. They call their scooter a 'cart.'

Joan: The first cart we had was an old Bronco. I bought it at a garage sale for practically nothing. It was in real bad condition. My husband fixed it up and he used it quite a bit before he sold it.

Tom: It had a solid–tire front wheel. You get on those streets like downtown Mountain View and you shake your teeth out! But it would go. Man, that thing would go! I pretty well wore out the first cart. The first two carts we had were secondhand.

Joan: Our first one, that Bronco, had a hydraulic seat. So you could raise the seat and take something down from a high shelf. That was in '87, I think it was. I started using a scooter because of water on my knee.

Tom: Then in August of '88 I had that stroke. I got a wheelchair. It rode good but it was so little I couldn't balance myself.

So I took over the cart. And she said, "You took my cart." And I said, "Well, I gave you a brand new car. The damn thing cost $21,000. What are you crying about? You want to trade? We'll trade!" (laughter) When her foot was bad she used it. The cart really won't go all the way up to Daly City. The car will. If you've got your credit cards at the gas pump, the car will go a long ways!

Joan: I take longer trips than he does! When my foot was bad, the only time I used the cart was like when you saw me downtown— where it's too far to walk, like Great America (an amusement park in San Jose). Our grandchildren wanted to go there. And so he gets in his wheelchair and grabs his cane and hooks it on the back of my cart and off we go—all over Great America like that.

Tom: We see people walking along and we come zipping by.

Joan: They look at us. And there was a whole group of policemen standing there and as we go by Tom says, "Can you believe she used to be a truck driver!"

I have heart trouble and my legs and body will only take me so far. I recently had three operations. I had a vein opened up in my chest, and they cut my neck and scraped that one out. And then I had my gallbladder out two weeks ago—through a catheter in the belly button. Can you imagine that? I came home the next day. I feel a lot better now.

Tom: They kept Joan overnight. And on the way home she said, "Let's stop and eat." She got a turkey sandwich with a bunch of lettuce on it. Something she hadn't eaten in a long time. And with no ill effects.

After we moved here to Mountain View the batteries got so that if I went as far downtown as I did the other day, I'd be creeping by the time I got home. So I went to buy new batteries. Sears charges about $60 a battery but at the scooter shop it's about $108. Sears didn't have them in stock but they had another battery which was bigger. So I bought two of them. Then I went all the way to Moffett Field to the Commissary and came all the way back home, still going like a bat out of hell!

Joan: They're much bigger batteries. These are wheelchair batteries.

Tom: They're heavy too. You can't pick them up so easy.

Joan: If you cannot walk, a three-wheel scooter's not the thing for you. Sometimes you have to put your foot out to catch yourself. With three wheels you can tip very easily on the curbs. If you cannot walk you should have four wheels. Like the ones they have in the market for customers to use; they are very wide.

Tom: They're better for a market because they're highly maneuverable and you're sitting up a little higher. In one of those huge baskets you can put $300–$400 worth of groceries, more than you can put in two ordinary shopping carts. We go over to Walmart and they've got them too.

Joan: Walmart also has a couple of employees that go around on a cart. And it looks like they can't walk, that they're handicapped.

Tom: Our grandson had a friend in school whose little sister was about eight years old, weighed about 45 or 50 pounds, and had a wheelchair that was very stylish. She would get her fingers on that little controller and you've never seen anything like it. You couldn't outrun her. A big grin on her face. I'm telling you, that girl got around. Their van would come to a stop, the door would open and out would come a lift. That little girl was down the lift and gone before you could get out of the front seat and get on the ground.

I've met a lot of people on the cart—carts attract people on canes, people on crutches. I see so many, especially retired guys down at the Navy base. Arthritis so bad and they're in their seventies, maybe World War II veterans. They're going along shaking, with a three-legged cane.

I ask them, "Why not buy one (scooter)?" They claim they cost too much money, but you can get 80% of it paid by Medicare and the other 20% you can get if you're on supplementary health care. If they have to pay for the scooter either they aren't 65 or they're not covered with Medicare B. There's a lot of those old veterans that could use a cart—like this Colt I have now made by the Lark Company.

Joan: We paid for ours. Of course we got ours at bargains. One from a garage sale, one my daughter bought from a private party. And then I was looking in the newspaper one day and here's this advertisement. Electric cart, new batteries and a charger for $500. The man had used it once or twice. He paid over $3000 for it.

Tom: A lot of people want to get rid of them.

Joan: It even had that orange flag. It hadn't been used at all. The molding on the tires wasn't even worn off.

Tom: One time I got hit on the cart in Palo Alto. The light for me was green, but this lady was coming up in her car and she stopped and looked at me. When she smiled and nodded I started to cross the street. And I'll be damned if she didn't start forward and hit me! Broke the plastic on the front end of the cart a little bit, made a big scrape in it and tore the arm. It didn't hurt me. Oh, I got a little brush burn.

Joan: I have tipped over going down curbs. If you head it straight on you can go up them. But with the three–wheel cart if you hit it at an angle (other than 'straight on') the thing will tip over.

Tom: I'll tell you an adventure she had. When we lived in Redwood City, Joan took the cart and went down to the little market. That's when her knee was bad, before I had the stroke. She called me up on the telephone, "I can't make this thing go; it just barely creeps; I don't know what to do." So I walked down there. One of the battery plugs had unplugged and she was running on only one battery.

Joan: No, it was the reset button.

Tom: Well, that's a different time. That was hilarious. It wasn't too long after that stroke. I couldn't walk far. It was about January or February. We went in the Hillsdale Shopping Center. All of a sudden the damn thing won't go. The tires were good. I checked all the plugs and it was just totally dead. So I pushed the thing from the Emporium back to Sears, about two blocks away.

It took me an hour and a half to get the cart back to the van. And I was really disgusted and discouraged. I was ready to kick the thing down a deep draw. By then I hurt so bad I just crawled in the van and sat there. Then we came home.

I rested up and got the cart out and took the thing apart to see what happened. Remember now, I'm an electrical engineer. On top of the battery is a little overload switch with a red button on it. If the button pops up it turns the machine off. You push it back down to reset it. What had happened is that a screw had come loose and the clamp under the front wheel got up against the battery terminal and shorted it out. I feel so stupid over that.

A lot of times I can get *off* a pretty good-sized curb, but I can't get *up* on one. Right in the middle of this block I could get up one driveway but I couldn't get off the sidewalk at the other end—no curb cut. So I was in the street. A policeman came up alongside me. He says, "Look, why don't you ride that thing on the sidewalk?"

And I lost my cool. The man was so smart-alecky. I says, "I'll tell you what officer, I'll ride it back to the corner there, you put the cart on the sidewalk, and I'll ride it to the next corner, and then you pick me up and put me on the street. You go with me!" He said, "Oh, I see what you mean." I haven't seen that officer since. That was in Redwood City.

Joan: One time I was riding the Lark at Letterman Hospital. People would stop me in the hallways and say, "Where did you get that? How much are they?" I had a real streamlined Lark at the time, the one with the hydraulic seat, the whole bit. The Lark company sent me brochures that I could hand out to people, but no way would they employ me. They didn't want me involved at all.

Tom: I'll tell you a little experience. There used to be a stretch on Broadway in Redwood City where the cars would race. I come around the corner one time and I see this policeman who's sitting way down there on his motorcycle. He's got his radar gun in his hand. I got right up even with him. He said, "Let's see, you were going 6.2 miles an hour!" He cracked me up! I said, "Really?" He said, "Well, that's what it says here!" And he got a big grin on his face. I said, "Well, that's good to know. I'm glad I wasn't breaking the speed limit."

Joan: My mother lived behind us in Redwood City. She's ninety-five next month and still living on her own. She had a knee replacement and all, but she has never driven a car all her life. And she has never had any desire to get on that cart.

Tom: We tried to get her to. If she was interested in it, why, we'd get her one. We've other family here too: a daughter in Sunnyvale and another one in Foster City. And five grandsons. The youngest one's adopted. He's ten now.

Joan: And he thinks the cart's a toy.

Tom: I get the biggest kick out of kids. You're going along and the little girls, they'll look at you, but they really don't want to get on that cart too much. But the little boys, you can see them itching. So, every once in a while I'll say, "Come here." I take a look at Mama because some of the mamas don't want you to do anything and I can't blame them for getting worried. Get the little boy up there and I tell him how it works. The kid is in stitches laughing with the biggest grin on his face driving this cart around. I take kids for a ride quite often. I love the kids. If God gave me the strength and money, I'd have kids all my life.

Joan: What I used the cart a lot for in Redwood City—I'd go garage 'sale-ing.' I can carry quite a bit on that cart. One thing I like about the Lark, it had a section in the back where I could put two gallons of milk.

Tom: This one has one too, but it's too small. So I made a little two-wheel trailer.

Joan: I don't think I've ever had a cart on behind me. The only thing I do is pull him in the wheelchair.

Tom: I like to ride the cart—in good weather. I go to the library a lot. I read everything I can get my hands on. After I recovered from the stroke, I got bored and I started reading. I went to the library in Redwood City so much, the people thought I worked there. I started writing too.

I wrote a poem and it got published—part of a contest. I came in honorable mention. I sent them two poems and the one that they gave me an honorable mention on I thought was the sorriest one of the two! It was the Poetic Society of America in Connecticut. They do that once a year. It's in a book in the library.

I went to Korea as a young man and I sometimes wonder how I came out of there. I suppose there's probably tens of thousands of other people that feel the same way. It's a piece of their life they wish they hadn't lived and wish they could get out of their minds. For many years I didn't talk about it. I would have dreams about it sometimes, very horrible dreams.

One day I started talking about it. I've had very few of these nightmares since. I'm convinced that that's the secret. So I sat down and wrote this other poem:

Life's Fulfillment

The band played a Sousa march as the men stood at attention,
No eyelids moved, no lip flickered as all stood there listening.
The hero, said the General, to all with hearts so proud,
He is a man we all respect, who will stand out in any crowd.
This man did do a wonderful deed, the General did declare,
He killed an enemy in combat, he is the man of the hour.
Yes, it's true that I had done this thing considered great,
But was it done with love of all or was it simply hate?
What about that young man killed, did a father lose a son,
Or did he die out there alone and loved by not a one.
Was he once a baby his mother thought the best?
Had she given him the breath of life and fed him from her breast?
I wonder if this young soldier who died there by my hand,
Had ever loved somebody back in his homeland?
I remember well that granite plate out upon that hill,
The memory of that awful day is with me even still.
Oh why men, young indeed, will live through terrible strife,
And bring such awful hurt into another person's life.
That adventure is now a memory of long, long ago,
Life is something now past that young enemy will never know.

I thought that was the best of the two poems. I'm not even a writer. I had never tried to write. I'm hyperactive. Attention deficit disorder. And I have dyslexia. Which means I turn letters around. It happens to me more in four-letter words like much, M–C–U–H. Why I do it I don't know, but I've done it all my life. With numbers too, I switch them around.

But I was master of a Masonic Lodge and we put out a journal each month. I've always felt like and sincerely believe that the printed word is more powerful than a sword. And if you don't believe it just consider people that will pay for ads. They wouldn't print them if it didn't pay. So the printed word is a terribly powerful tool. I like to tell stories and I wrote in the journal every month. I wanted something to get people thinking. That's what got me started writing.

Another thing that got me writing, one time right after I had that stroke, I was sitting in my chair. I was reading a magazine that had what I considered the sorriest piece of trash called writing that ever was. I got disgusted and I said, "You know, anybody can write a better article than that. Even me!"

And Joan says, "Prove it." I wrote a lot of instruction manuals in the working years, but that's strictly 'how to.' How to drive a car. One, open the door. Two, get in it!

But this is another thing. She said, "Why don't you write about when you were a kid in the Ozarks?" One of my journal editors said, "Tom, the Titanic was built by experts, people who were trained engineers, architects, and experienced people. Noah's Ark was built by an amateur." I got the message!

Joan: I'm sure he read it somewhere.

Tom: So I started writing. And I must have had about 210,000 words and I kept going to it and editing and editing and editing. And I got it down now to where I believe it's about 70,000 words and 500 pages. I think it's readable. It might not be worth a damn, but it's readable. So I took it to the post office. I sent it to a press in New York.

I got such a kick out of writing it. Every person in it has a real-life counterpart. Maybe not for his entire life, but at least for some of it. It is fiction really. I call it *The End of Neighborhood Innocence*.

Fiction is tough to get published. Next to impossible. Some houses will do it if you'll pay the publishing price. If they come back and want $3000 for publishing, I'm not going to do it! If they want $400 or $500 dollars I'll let them do it. We'll see.

VI.

Men on Their Own

Donald: Oklee Maluna

Tom: Always Doing Something

Donald Sauer

Donald Sauer

**"I've seen too many people down and very depressed.
Depression is worse to me than cancer
because it affects you up here (pointing to his head)...
When I was in the hospital I didn't die,
so now I'm going to enjoy this world; I'm going to enjoy my life."**

Donald Sauer was cruising a Palo Alto, California street fair on his scooter when I first met him. He spoke with me later in his apartment at Casa Olga, in downtown Palo Alto.

Donald first moved to Casa Olga after a hospital stay in 1988— following an auto accident, months of frustration with the courts, and drinking that he said damaged his health.

Initially he was in an intermediate care apartment where there is assisted living that provides meals, a cleaning service, and personal care.

Then Donald had a laryngectomy for throat cancer in 1991. When his health and independence improved, he moved to a residential apartment in 1992—where he was living when I interviewed him.

"After I was in the hospital for the throat surgery, they wouldn't turn me loose to go back to my own place; they sent me here to assisted living in Casa Olga. My condition at the time was caused by me—too much whiskey.

"I damaged my liver and my balance is gone now. I don't really notice any other problems from drinking. I usually take a glass full of milk thistle extract every morning. It helps your liver. Because of the amount of beer that I drink, I figure my liver does need a little protection.

"For a while after I came here from the hospital, a friend helped me get around; but she was leaving shortly. One day I saw an ad for a scooter in one of the papers. I'd been getting around pretty good but I figured I had the money, so I might as well buy a scooter—even though Medicare wouldn't pay for it. The scooter is made by Electric Mobility. It says right on it: MADE WITH PRIDE IN THE USA IN SEWELL, NEW JERSEY. I have baskets attached, front and back.

"I mainly use the scooter to go to the stores. It takes me about 25 minutes to get there. Sometimes I think people wonder why a young guy like me is using this thing. I am almost 60—three more years. How could a guy my age be in a scooter already? But I try to dress nice and everything.

"When I had the laryngectomy for throat cancer, I lost my voice box so I have an artificial larynx. They cut the vocal cord on the right side—you have two cords; one on each side. The artificial larynx mixes up the vibrations in there and turns them into sounds.

"It will work for you too," he told me. "You hold it up to the throat and just use your mouth and form the words in your throat. You don't make the sound; just press the button."

I tried to use the voice box as Donald instructed. The only results were a kind of strangled 'arghhh.'

"It takes some practice. Even I sometimes miss a word. Watch my lips too. It's easier indoors with no other noises. Some people understand me right away, and there are others that say, 'What did you say? What did you say?' I get back at them though. I just turn off the sound and cuss at them.

"After I recovered from the surgery and got my independence, I moved up here into this apartment. And I've got the prettiest room on these two floors, with a good view of the mountains. They clean the room once a week, but I don't need any other help. I don't take any medications. I use the beer to keep my throat moist. Beer's not really a friend. It's a companion. I've always enjoyed drinking my beer. At this point, it is one of my few enjoyments.

"Now that I'm not in assisted living, I don't eat in the dining room. If I decide to have a salad or braised corn—because I love that—I eat what I want. I cook whatever is easy right here in the apartment. I make all my own choices whatever I do here.

"Everybody here at Casa Olga wants to help me on and off the elevator but they get in my way. I wish they would just get out of my way. I do everything myself. I am really independent."

There was a bird in a cage in Donald's living room and I asked him about it.

"I got this bird for my birthday from my brother. My sister-in-law had come up from Nevada. She sells birds and had about three or four with her—different colors. Right away I went over to the yellow bird and said, 'I want to take her.' She's a miniature cockatoo.

"I got a Hawaiian name for the bird: Oklee Maluna. That means Little Bottoms Up! I have a good sense of humor. The manager here is from Hawaii, a real nice lady. She told me what bottoms up is in Hawaiian, gave me the translation.

"I've had the bird about three years. She hasn't been able to tell me yet how old she is, but she may be trying." Speaking to the bird, 'I know you want your cage cleaned. I'll do that in a minute. Go ahead. Spit it out! I've got another female in my room and you're jealous.'

"Once in a while I let her out of the cage since it is pretty small. Once she tried to fly out the window and went right into the pane. I don't want her to hurt herself. You have to become a Daddy to 'em.

"I take the bird out for a walk once in a while to get some sunshine. I hang her cage on my walker. I have no place to hold her cage on the scooter, but I will get something figured out. I've been trying to teach her to talk too, but she hasn't learned yet. She's got a birdbrain."

I asked Donald how he spends his time.

"Before I retired, I did enjoy my work. Because I was the best in my field. I was a form carpenter, a foundation man. One of the best in the Valley. That's the truth. I'm not trying to brag. If you don't love yourself, ain't nobody else to love you.

"I don't do anything much any more, but I only sleep about four or five hours a night. I am up from early in the morning 'til after midnight and it's hard for me to go back to sleep. So I watch television. I like Hogan's Heroes. Sometimes when I wake up or can't sleep, I turn that on.

"I've been looking around every once in a while, trying to find a gal who wants to play cards; I like to play Rummy and Cribbage. But most people are either very depressed, or they are not that talented, or they've got Alzheimer's or something.

"I read, too, mostly the newspapers, sex books, and some robberies and murders—the same old thing every day. My eyes are getting bad, though large print helps. And I use glasses when I read; things come clearer.

"I don't have to hurry anymore. And I don't want to fall down. I just try to relax and behave myself, have a few beers and make sure I have enough to eat.

"But I got nobody. I'm really one of these shy guys. I could be gone tomorrow. You never know. I still worry about my cancer. If I got it I got it. I'm living with it. When I was in the hospital I didn't die, so now I'm going to enjoy this world; I'm going to enjoy my life.

"I've seen too many people down and very depressed. Depression is worse to me than cancer because it affects you up here (pointing to his head). Everybody around here can't figure out why I always have a smile on my face. I tell them I am drinking the right kind of beer.

"I try to keep a smile on my face. I think it's helped a few of the people here. They see me, and pretty soon they start smiling. Good humor rubs off. I'm better than a frown—it looks a hell of a lot better.

"I wake up with a smile every morning. I'm alive and enjoy the day. The more I appreciate everything I do, the more the world looks beautiful. I look at the good things and everything to me now is beautiful. Everything."

Tom Churchwell

Tom Churchwell

**"It's a little hard to be creative now because I can't work with my hands any more. I do try to express it though...
Sometimes I think it's through the carts I've built. I really do!"**

As with most of the people whose stories appear in this book, I first met Tom riding along the streets of Mountain View on what he calls his 'cart,' referring to its similarity to golf carts. Later, I interviewed him in his mobile home.

"I started building carts in 1987 because I couldn't drive a car after I had a stroke," he began. "I have some of my eyesight back now, but I'm considered legally blind. I'm not a dependent person and it was hard to get around. So I threw a three–wheel bicycle together. I dumpster dive, use anything and everything I can find.

"I have made a lot of these carts." (See the top photo on the left for the first cart he made after the stroke.) "I can put groceries in all those baskets on the back; just built on a bike. I found out you could get an electric motor for it. I've taken off most of the decoration now, and I'm just getting ready to redo it again. I get ideas, start over again, and do it better.

"The one I use now (pictured with Tom on it) is a heavy duty guy, more of a golf cart really. I've been south to San Jose and north to

San Mateo; that's about the farthest—which is not bad. It runs about eighteen miles an hour, has a fifty-mile radius.

"I've also made one or two carts for other people. One for a young man from Vietnam. He had been a friend of mine for quite some time, a kid about fourteen years old. He got interested because the cart reminded him of Vietnam, though he was only about four when he left his home country.

"I was peddling along one day, and he happened to stop me. Wanted to know how I built the cart. First it was powered by pedal, and then I got an electric motor for it. It had a handle to regulate the electricity and the batteries were back underneath. If you're handy you can put just about anything together. I actually built his so he could pedal it rickshaw-like. He had a top on it and stands that folded out. He would go over to the school grounds, sell candy, and made extra money off the darn thing."

Somehow the rickshaw story made me wonder about earlier parts of Tom's life.

"I've been married twice. Now I'm separated, and I've lived here in the trailer about three years. Before this, I took care of my mother for some time. Then she passed away and I took care of my father when he got ill. I was with my father at the time I had the stroke in 1987.

"I don't have any children of my own, but I 'adopted' half the kids in the neighborhood. My 'adopted' grandson Travis started coming up to the house just after the stroke, and he just kind of worked himself in. My stepfather hated kids, but he liked Travis. And Travis just loved Mom's dog. The dog didn't like anybody, but he got along with Travis. So you know he had a good heart. I used to take Travis around on the cart. He was four or five years old. Now he's getting older, he don't want to drive it.

"I also used to work with kids through the Mountain View Police Department. Usually they were not bad kids, just mischievous— that's what I would say. I'd take kids out on field trips, and I enjoyed it. I like kids. I always have. Being a Big Brother I guess is what you would call it. We used to take kids up to San Francisco, over to Mount Tamalpais, and up in through the wine country and the hot springs. I did have a good time. I was young then, and I liked to hike. I was a good hiker.

"There was a write-up about my work with kids in the Mountain View paper in about May or June of 1990. I was taking the kids up to Rengstorff Park, where the newspaper took pictures for the interview. Now it's just Jason, my foster son; he lives here. He'll be going back to school and into the National Guard.

"I was in the Navy myself—from '50 to '57. I enjoyed it. I really got to travel. I've been from the South Pole to the North Pole. I was in Korea. I've been up off the Aleutian Islands for a rescue mission. I've been everywhere: Australia, New Zealand, New Guinea, Borneo... all through the South Pacific, every one of the Marshall Islands, all the little bitty ones. The islands are beautiful.

"I was supposed to be on a world tour cruise. We got three-quarters of the way through when we had to go pick up an admiral down at the South Pole. It's the coldest place I've ever been in all my life! I don't want to ever go there anymore.

"After the Navy—during the '60s—I used to make jewelry and wax carve. I made rings and stuff like that. Back in the hippie days on Haight-Ashbury, a bunch of us went together and started to open shops. We had unusual items that you couldn't get anywhere else. It was kind of communal, but everybody did their own thing. I did enjoy it; It was fun.

"Later on it got out of hand, too much of a drug scene. But at the beginning it was entirely different. They may have smoked a little grass. I know I did myself. But the flower children were just love and peace. The hippies—the name came from HIP: Haight-Ashbury International Proprietors.

"One thing that's hard on me now is that I've always been very active. It just hit me all at once to have a stroke at 55. Now I can't do all that much. I don't have the proper use of this hand. My vision was impaired. I can't read because I can't stay on the lines. I also had trouble spelling. I managed to come back quite a bit, but they didn't think it was worth sending me back to school to get caught up in computers."

So Tom did not get retrained for work he might do after the stroke, perhaps because he was within less than ten years of retirement.

"A year after the stroke, I was hit by a car and had a concussion. Now it's very hard to function and think, hard to get my words at times. The lawyer I had to defend me let my case go until the very end, and then he wanted me to take over. I couldn't get another lawyer. I was sick and had to go to the hospital. So I lost out. I'll never forget that lawyer, the blond curly-haired guy on TV.

"My mind is muddled now and I have epileptic seizures; the medication for it, Dilantin, made my gums shrink and I had to have all my teeth pulled within a year.

"I had already broken my neck and back in '61 in a car accident, so I've been going through this for years, in and out of a wheelchair and using crutches. It's nothing new, but it has just been a hard time over the years.

"I want to go as long as I can. I just wish I could do some other things. I would like to be able to go sky diving or skin diving or hang gliding. Off the cliffs down there by Half Moon Bay...but it's too cold anyhow.

"I've got plenty of time to do things. I built the carts, and now I ride them around and I shop. When I go into a store, I've got a grocery cart to hang on to. I usually get by with that pretty well. The carts in the store that you can sit in are for people worse off than I am. That's the way I feel. As long as I can use my legs, I will!

"I like going out on Shoreline Boulevard. Sometimes I like to take a ride up to Stanford and look through the museums, but it's a little too far now; it's just getting too hard on me.

"I can walk around here at home. But every now and then my legs just quit; I have to make sure I can grab ahold of something. I can only walk about a block. I've got the pool and the sauna here, and I go swimming. It's good therapy. Usually I've got a lot of doctors' appointments! That keeps me busy right there!

"I use the three-wheeler to go to the Chanwell Clinics on Castro Street. I can get the help that I need right away. Sometimes I stop at a coffee shop along the way and have a coffee. Just go where I feel like going. I meet a lot of people. I'm gabby.

"It's a little hard to be creative now because I can't work with my hands any more. I do try to express it though...Sometimes I think it's through the carts I've built. I really do!"

VII.

Related Diagnoses
Unique Lives

Kay: Always Someone There

Mary: Learning to Change

Katherine (Kay)
Heller

Katherine (Kay) Heller

**"You can modify your life. Just think about it...
and there has always been somebody there (for me).
You develop faith in the whole world."**

Kay was having lunch in a bagel shop in Mountain View, California when I first met her. She had ridden her scooter there from her apartment in Sunnyvale, a few miles away. Some days later, I interviewed her in her home.

"I started my career as a nurse and then became a social worker. Before I was disabled, I worked in a program for handicapped kids in San Mateo County. I even worked as a substitute teacher *after* I had the scooter—in an Adult Education program running parent groups. We were supposed to get people who had been on welfare for years and solve all those social problems in six months.

"After 1960 I was aware of increasing disability. I found out that I had rheumatoid arthritis and rather severely deteriorating joints from osteoarthritis. My sister and brother are arthritic and a cousin has similar problems. But nobody else in the family uses a scooter.

"I had a great many surgeries to treat the arthritis. They said I would be laid up for four operations in two years. It's actually been ten years and seventeen operations. My shoulders were replaced totally last year—which is great because they were miserably painful before. I have better range of motion in my shoulders now, but I have to lift one arm with the other; one won't do it alone. My neck and hands have been fused. I didn't comb my hair for a long time. I get it cut short in the back and get a perm. You can modify your life. Just think about it.

"After six surgeries, my ankles were finally fused. They had to put a rod up my right leg. It doesn't bend now; I can't use it at all. I also have some nerve damage and I don't really know where that right foot is in space. I have to look down when I'm walking and then I lose my balance. The surgery took away the pain but it didn't do much for my independence. The left foot is better; the only motion missing is side to side. No way could I pick myself up off the floor by pushing with my feet. And if I step on a pebble, I'm down because the whole foot rolls over.

"I was in two long-leg casts and a wheelchair at one point. I lived in a mobile home, so for a few months I couldn't get out because of the steps.

"Then during one period of sitting, a multi-county service called Outreach helped me with transportation. You put $25 or $50 dollars on deposit and they draw against it as you use the service. They're available twenty-four hours a day. One time they took me at five o'clock in the morning with my niece and nephew—they called them attendants—and their golf stuff to the airport. They didn't consider it an imposition.

"I'm better now than I've been for years really. I don't hurt like I did when I was running around trying to climb the Sierra mountains. And I still have my hips, my own hair, my own teeth, and one eye!

"Until recently, I was managing the sixty-two-piece South Bay Community Orchestra. Then my neck fell apart. I discovered the strain was too much, that I couldn't do it any more. The orchestra is really good, and I want to do an article on them; I'm taking a writing course now.

"And I have always loved to travel. I wanted kids, but I had everybody else's kids including my nieces and nephews. They thought I was the best thing since ice cream because I could take them traveling. One spring vacation I took my brother's three to Washington, DC and we did the works.

"What an experience! One boy and two girls. The girls wanted to see things in the Smithsonian like the First Ladies' gowns. The boy's interest was different but they all loved the mint. We were upset because, where we could see the printing process, the money was printed on only one side.

"We did Gettysburg battlefield on our hands and knees. My nephew wanted to find a bullet. And he thought there must be some bloody dirt somewhere. He knew all about one general who had his leg amputated on the battle field, and he knew the leg was somewhere in the Smithsonian. We finally found the leg and he fainted dead away!

"Even *with* the arthritis, I still went places. I went to Switzerland with two friends, a cast on one leg, and the other one not very functional. I had forearm Canadian crutches but no scooter. We used trains and small planes. We flew from Finland over the coast of Norway. It was like seeing the earth developing because it was so primitive and down to basic rock. We had a wonderful time. This was in about 1986.

"Then after I retired I did the perimeter of the country in a trailer with one of these same friends. Out to Prince Edward Island and everywhere. A trailer is a good way as long as you can get into it; you can stop anytime you want. I could shimmy into the front seat and I had hand controls so I could drive without needing my feet. I didn't have a scooter but I had the wheelchair. My friend could push me when we went to museums since I couldn't walk any real distance.

"I kept admiring scooters! By 1988, the Canadian crutches were wearing out my shoulders and I wasn't using the wheelchair much. I said to the doctor, 'Why not a scooter?' I have a wonderful, wonderful rheumatologist at Kaiser, Dr. Tom Barrens. He wrote out a prescription right off the bat. I had one scooter for seven years and I've had this one for two.

"As soon as I got the prescription, I went looking for a scooter right away. I had the wheelchair in the car and I could wheel the chair backwards pretty well with one foot. It drove everybody nuts, but not me! I think they thought I was a loose bomb. Anyway I found exactly the scooter I wanted.

"The first scooter I had was a Pace Saver. It was like a solid gold Cadillac to me! You could raise and lower the seat eight inches or more with a hydraulic lift—which made a substantial difference. I could reach the oranges in Safeway. I don't need it any more now that my shoulders don't hurt, but at the time reaching was very painful—even just feeding myself. Medicare refused to cover the cost of the hydraulic seat but Senior Adult Legal Assistance fought the battle for me. It helped to know the system!

"The first scooter was Maria. She exactly matched the beige upholstery on my car at the time. So I said the car must have been pregnant. I got it at Abbey's, where they gave me the Kaiser discount. But they wouldn't take assignment—which means that they wait until Medicare pays them before they reimburse you. It wasn't too easy to lay out the money up front. Even though I had retired from a very good job as a social worker, I had my mother in a nursing home for three years. I didn't have too much savings accumulated.

"Medicare paid 80% of what they thought I should have paid. My supplementary Kaiser insurance paid the difference up to $1900, and I paid the rest, $300. It was a very manageable thing. Medicare and Kaiser take care of replacement batteries and there's very little maintenance.

"I just have trouble keeping fifty pounds of air in the tires. I can tell when I need my tires pumped up because although the battery's charged, the scooter is still dragging. It goes four plus miles an hour—a fast walk. You can adjust the speed from zero to full blast. I keep forgetting to turn down the full blast when I get to the front door and I come charging into the house! That wall where I usually park was a terrible mess once!

"Winston is the new scooter, the Pace Saver Excel. I've bought a sun shade for it since I'm on prescription gold for the rheumatoid arthritis and I have to stay out of the sun. At first I didn't believe that and I sunned myself up at Tahoe. I fried!! I got the new scooter at Rehab Specialists in Mountain View. They make home visits and they took assignment on the scooter, so I didn't have to pay up front.

"I also have a Bruno Jr. lift. This is the third car the lift has been on. When you get a new car the manufacturer will reimburse you to transfer the lift and hand controls. Neither do you pay taxes on them because they're medical equipment.

"The lift cost about $1000 and Medicare doesn't pay for that. They don't mind buying a scooter, but I guess they don't expect you to be driving or gainfully employed, which is sort of silly.

"Also, the scooter has a weight limit. I have a nephew-in-law who would love to take a ride, but I think he weighs over 250 pounds. I don't know what the limit is. I have seen scooters advertised that carry up to 300 pounds. I got up to 220 when I was sitting around, which was terrible. I've gotten back to 140 and I need to take off another ten.

"When I went out in the wheelchair everybody looked at me like, 'Oh, you poor thing. What can I do for you?' You're sort of tempted to sit there and look pitiful. Or even to think maybe you *are* pitiful. I didn't get too much of that in a wheelchair because I'm too talkative.

"On the other hand, when I was in the wheelchair, the grocery store people would take the bags down from shelves because I couldn't reach them. With the scooter they seem to be thinking, 'That looks easy,' and they let me help myself.

"When you're in a scooter however, society greets you like an able person . They don't talk to you like you probably don't understand very well. The scooter is just magnificent!

"When I go shopping, I drive the van with the scooter in the back and then take the scooter out when I get to the store. Except when I go for groceries. Then I don't even *take* the scooter. I use the one they have in the store. They load the groceries into the van, and when I get home I've got the scooter handy to take the stuff into the house.

"The scooter makes friends all over the place. The key thing all folks ask is, 'Where did you get it? How did you get it?' And I tell them all about Medicare and that if they're on MediCal it pays for most of it. Kids all want to ride it but I won't let them. Haven't they got a scooter? Yes they have. So I say, 'Well, that's for you and this is for me.' And the dogs water my wheels! They come up and they sniff around and then they own me! (laughter)

"One time I was going across Central Expressway at Mary Avenue in Sunnyvale, and the scooter died right in the middle of the street. Everyone stopped and got out of their cars and wanted to push me, scooter and all, because I couldn't even stand up. But all of that worked smoothly; it was lovely. There has always been somebody there. You develop faith in the whole world.

"The least likely to help you are the well-dressed yuppies. They're on their way to some important something or other. I think they're going to change when they're a little older. When something hurts.

"As far as stability goes, I've only tipped over once and that was up in the gold country in Virginia City. It's all boardwalks and hilly and lumpy. I think I approached a curb on the diagonal when I probably should have faced it head—on—at a right angle. The diagonal is not a good way in the three–wheeler. And it has small wheels in the back, which eliminates your access to places somebody could tip you up onto if you were in a wheelchair. On a scooter, you have to find a cut in the sidewalk or a driveway.

"It's not so hot in sand of course! It isn't something that you can take to the beach. But I used a beach chair on the sand; I turned it around backwards and walked right into the water with it!

"If there is a really steep place where I have to go downhill in the scooter, I have to zigzag. But I avoid that if possible. Very few places now don't have access or a ramp of some sort. Rest rooms is a different story!

"Cupertino High School doesn't have a bathroom for the handi-capped. I went to that bathroom once and thought I was there for life. It had a low seat and there wasn't anything to grab, absolutely nothing. Finally I pulled myself up using the scooter. But it's not very safe; if I pull high on it, it will move because I'm bigger than it is. I could write a travel guide on rest rooms!

"I've never tried a four-wheeler. It seems to me it would be harder to fit into the van. The mini-van I have now, a Summit Eagle, has the gear shift on the floor. Both brakes and gas are on the side of the steering column, which is fun. I have a hard time getting up into the van, but it's good exercise. I can't take anybody in the back seats when I am carrying the scooter. If I have four people I take the old wheelchair that folds up, and when we do a lot of walking they can push me.

"Another help was when the doctor gave me a prescription for two bedrooms and two baths. He says I need an attendant. And I'm on a HUD subsidy. I only pay $363 for an $1800 apartment. There's room enough for everything I need and there's a washer and dryer. A cleaning lady comes about twice a month.

"I did spend some time in a nursing home once. Never again. Somebody came in the first night and whipped off my covers to put on a diaper. I said, 'I'm not incontinent,' but he put them on automatically every night. They apologized that I was in a room with somebody who was senile. But Maggie wasn't senile; the battery in her hearing aid was dead. I told her daughter she needed a new battery."

Kay had been talking about going to church. I asked her how faith has been a significant part of the way she approaches life.

"I'm a Catholic convert. When I was in my twenties, I had my appendix out—two weeks before I finished nursing training. I had an infection afterwards that lasted about five years. It kept getting abscesses that had to be drained. They thought I had Hodgkin's disease, and in those days you were not going to be around long with that.

"The Protestant churches I had been exposed to didn't work for me, but I was always sort of aware of an uncaused cause. I needed to connect with it somewhere. Every time I got tired, I'd go down into the pits again. I couldn't find an answer.

133

"At the time I became a Catholic I was teaching Unitarian Sunday School on Sunday morning, going to the Episcopal Church at night, and trying to figure out how I felt about Jesus. You know, he said he was the son of God. Was he or wasn't he? He was a liar or wasn't he?

"And then, I don't know, all of a sudden I needed something that said, 'This is the truth,' instead of 'Make up your own mind.' I knew there was an uncaused cause and that whatever it was, it was bigger than we are. You'll go crazy if you try to think of who caused God.

"I just suddenly said to somebody, 'I'm going to become a Catholic.' Then I nearly swallowed my tongue. I don't know how that came out of my mouth. It really was like the Holy Ghost hit me. And I wanted to say, 'Go away!' Because I came from a WASP (White Anglo-Saxon Protestant) family. Off the Mayflower and all that. Very, very Protestant. But the Catholic Church works fine for me. And I love the parish here—Saint Cyprian's; it's the best church I've ever been in.

Mary
Ramirez

Mary Ramirez

"When you grasp the concept of the possibility of changing, you feel a freedom that you weren't aware of before."

Mary Ramirez lives in San Jose, California. I met her on a rainy spring evening on her scooter behind the United Way office, where she was doing volunteer work. She agreed to an interview later in her home.

"I've had problems with rheumatoid arthritis for more than twenty years. The arthritis was always active, but I was able to walk and work. Nobody could tell there was anything wrong. It first seriously limited my mobility in 1991 when it affected the knee joint so badly that I didn't have a normal gait anymore.

"I couldn't get out of bed. The doctor saw my knees and said I needed a joint replacement. But I've kind of avoided that. Eventually I might need it, but it's better to put it off as long as you can. I've been getting good medical care through Valley Medical Center.

"I'm trying to keep the rheumatoid under control with medication. I try one medication for as long as it works; then I go on to something else. A few didn't do anything for me. Now I'm on something new and it's strong. It takes a few months to take effect, and you have to be monitored frequently because these are potent drugs.

"I was working until 1991 when I became disabled. I was doing clerical, reception, and front office work. I've been in accounting, after getting a community college degree. I was also in occupational therapy for a while. I took night school classes to learn about medical problems. Then I worked as an assistant in occupational therapy with people on disability. My education has been useful with volunteer work as well.

"Before I stopped working, I was doing some volunteer work for Stanford—research on arthritis. In 1991 when my knee was affected so badly, I had to drop out. I was walking up until then. After that everything went haywire.

"You have remissions and then flair-ups. The disease is systemic and progressive and there's really no cure yet. The main objective is to keep it under control and slow it down.

"I *was* driving, but it was difficult and I only drove when I had to. Then I was accidentially broad-sided. Luckily, I wasn't injured, just tossed around. But my car was totaled and I decided, 'This is it; no more driving!'

"From then on I pursued new means of transportation! I was getting around with a cane and taking the bus for a while. Little by little I started looking into wheelchairs, scooters and things. I did a lot of research, and I finally made my decision. But it's not easy; it's just like buying a car.

That's how I got this Bravo scooter. I've had it for two years. It's been a big learning experience. Like practicing to drive a car, you don't learn overnight. You make mistakes at first, learning all the little ins and outs. And it can be dangerous; you have to be careful. There aren't very many of us out there on scooters yet, so people aren't aware of what this is all about. We need some legislation for cars and scooters on the road.

"I got my scooter through an ad in the weekly *Potpourri*. I purchased it used, but it was actually brand new, and it's worked out fairly well for me. You can't do much if you can't get around. So it's a great aid to independence and doing little tasks that somebody else would have to do for you otherwise.

"I use it to go to the grocery store. I hang the bags on the scooter arms or put them down on the floor. I get out, get a little exercise, and move around; I'm not stuck indoors all the time. I think that helps a lot.

"I've taken the scooter on the bus and the light rail. I've been on the train as far as Santa Cruz and San Francisco, but I usually don't go that far by myself. I go with a travel guide, through the Escort Outreach program.

"You have to qualify for the service, and you make an appointment in advance. They come and pick you up, either by cab or in a van with a lift if you're wheelchair bound. I rely on Escort during the winter because it's a big struggle for me to get outdoors in the rain. It's a good service.

"Another thing I like to do, I love going to museums. I love art. There are so many things I really enjoy doing that I can still do.

"We have a lot of good things going on right here in San Jose. I like outdoor activities on the scooter, going to festivities downtown like the Symphony in the Park. I don't need anybody to push me around. I think the scooter's fantastic.

"Right now I also do flower arranging—as a hobby. It keeps me busy and creative since I can't do the things I used to do. I was really active. It's difficult for me to travel now, so I don't do that anymore; that's bygone. And I used to be very athletic; that's bygone too. But I've done those things.

"I had to slack off reading for some years, but I'm starting to read again. I like biographies and autobiographies and things about other cultures, foreign countries. Anything that's educational and worthwhile. I try to read foreign languages. Perhaps I'll get into some volunteer work with a foreign language.

"I was working for the Volunteer Exchange as a referral specialist. They have a data base listing hundreds of agencies that need volunteers. And we get calls from young and old who want to volunteer. We try to match them up, let people know what opportunities are available and give them several referrals.

"I think it's fantastic. Volunteering has helped me so much, just getting out and being able to feel I'm contributing and learning something new. It brings people closer together. Helps people understand something in a different field or another lifestyle.

"This place where I live is something new too. It's all single occupancy. Everyone is either working or retired or disabled, like myself—a variety of men and women. We each rent a room and share the kitchen and bathrooms. We have an offsite manager who comes in. And we try to keep it up. It's not like having a house of your own or an apartment where you have total privacy.

"But your rent is down. People come here for a while and then they move on. I guess there's going to be more of this with housing in short supply and so costly. This is a model for a different style of living.

"We have a pretty good group here. It's not easy living so close, you know. But if you get the right mix of people, it can work. This is actually a house so it's not soundproof like apartments. You hear every little noise. Mostly everybody is considerate; they don't use the washer in the middle of the night!

"But when you first move in, it's all new and you make mistakes. You begin to realize there are other people around, and little by little you catch on. I've been here two years, one of the longest. It was still under construction when I came. At first there were only about half a dozen of us. Now there are eighteen people here.

"I do have family in Santa Clara. I'm a California native and I've lived in this county all my life. My Mom is still alive. My Dad passed on in 1990. I have one married brother, a niece and a nephew. I have other relatives too—here and in Southern California.

"I haven't been able to see much of them because it's hard for me to get out or do too much in one day. And they are busy. I talk to them on the phone, but I don't really visit people very much, even my friends. I see the people here. It kind of feels like family; you're with these people all the time.

"I'm also very interested in the future evolution of new treatments for diseases like mine. With all the new technology, there are going to be many wonderful treatments to prevent major health problems. I'm kind of a guinea pig, I guess. I'm being treated by Stanford residents. They can learn from the people they see and treat.

"Even if they can't cure you, if your quality of life improves through drug treatment I think that's great. Contain pain, keep active, keep in the mainstream of society: that's the whole thing. Twenty or thirty years ago, people like me were put away somewhere. We aren't doing that anymore—because of new technology like the scooter, and medicine, and people's changing attitudes.

"Since people are living longer now, everybody's going to be disabled in some way if they live to be old! You're going to have some kind of health problem in your life! A lot of fantastic changes are going to happen. Diseases may be prevented or cured.

"There used to be so much negativity toward alternative forms of therapy or medical aid; but it's changing. Early on, I went against a lot of my doctors and did different things to help myself. I said, 'I'm having acupuncture and it's helping the pain.' They're beginning to realize that a lot of things besides traditional medicine help you.

"I used to swim too, before they had any water therapy programs. But I always did it on my own because I was athletic. And there are a lot of support groups. I belong to the Arthritis Foundation; I've been to support groups.

"I was doing a lot of reading on my own before I got into medical treatment. I used to read self–help books. It is up to people to be motivated to help themselves. You can't expect the medical profession to do it all. There has to be communication and working together. Little by little people are becoming educated. They realize they have to be responsible for their own health care needs, and not just let somebody else take care of them.

"I'm in a totally different frame of mind than I was a few years back; I was feeling really miserable then. Now even when I'm miserable, I know that I'm miserable. I might have a setback. But now I feel I can cope with it because there's going to be something that will help me if I just give it a chance. That's the way I have to think now.

"Everybody has ups and downs. If you don't have quality of life you can think, 'Why should I live?' You don't actually act on it, but we all think about it. And you're taught that it's a terrible thing.

"You read about Dr. Kavorkian and about all these people that are not happy and want to get out of this world. There's so much controversy now in that area! And it is sad. Especially if they leave loved ones behind. I guess there's guilt on both sides. I don't know. I don't see anything wrong with it if a person is suffering so badly that they do want to go. I don't know how I would feel if I got to the point that I couldn't take it anymore.

"I don't feel like that now. But if I hadn't gotten the medical help that I've been getting for the last several years, I don't know if I'd want to be around. That's what I mean about my change in attitude and thinking.

"I don't feel the things I'm telling you right now are any different than anybody else. I read about people who are in my predicament and I say, 'Hey, I'm not the only one that's going through this.' If we communicate we know we're not alone!

"I like to get out and be part of society. I don't feel that people who have disabilities should be kept hidden or sheltered. They should try to remain independent and be accepted. Let people know that you have the same feelings they do.

"I learned a lot about adaptive behavior in occupational therapy classes. I think that's what has helped me cope. People need to be educated about how to change. People don't want to change, but you have to. We're always changing actually, but I guess we don't realize it.

"You can learn ways of adapting and thinking about the future: 'I'm going to have to make a change so I'm going to have to learn new ways.' I'm always looking for something that's going to help me accomplish whatever I need to accomplish.

"As I progress to different stages, I go into different levels of activities. You learn how to find solutions to help you cope and make you feel better. That's all you can do! When you grasp the concept of the possibility of changing, you feel a freedom that you weren't aware of before. I don't know if you know what I'm talking about.

"We confine ourselves, I think. It's amazing people manage the feats that they do. It's inspiring. When you see what somebody else can accomplish, it gives you the motivation to try to hang in there. That's the whole thing.

"Think happy. You're not going to feel as bad because you're not going to dwell on your problem. I find that helps me a lot, an awful lot. But people don't realize that, you know. Even healthy people don't realize that."

Glossary of medical terms

Anterior Compartment Muscles—a group of muscles on the outside of the lower leg next to the skin. They pull the foot up toward the knee and prevent the foot from dragging when walking (called 'foot drop').

Ankle-Foot Orthotics—appliances such as braces or shoe inserts. They are used to support the ankle-foot joint, to prevent or correct deformities, and to improve the function of the joint.

Aorto-Femoral Bypass—a section of vein, or suitable substitute, grafted between the aortal and femoral arteries in the lower torso, to bypass an obstruction in an artery.

Artificial Larynx—an electro-mechanical voice box that makes sounds used in speech. It is used to replace a removed larynx, usually by surgery.

Attention Deficit Disorder—a condition characterized by decreased attention span, and often by hyperactivity and impulsive behavior.

Autonomic Dysreflexia—a syndrome (group of symptoms) including sudden excessively high blood pressure, caused by uncontrolled impulses from the sympathetic nervous system (the fight or flight system). People with spinal cord injuries are particularly at risk for this problem, considered a medical emergency.

Carotid Endartectomy—the surgical removal of deposits from the inner surface of the main artery in the neck to improve the circulation of blood to the head.

Claudication—pain in the limbs, especially the legs, caused by blocked blood vessels, during activity such as walking and usually relieved with rest.

Colonoscopy—examination of the lower digestive tract with a flexible tube fitted with a scope to see the tract walls and contents.

Isometrics—muscle contraction (tightening) without much change in muscle length, thus holding a part of the body still, but not relaxed. For example, holding the lower leg straight in the air while sitting down.

Laryngectomy—surgical removal of the upper part of the windpipe, often in conjunction with the use of an artificial larynx (see previous page).

Magnetic Resonance Imagery (MRI)—a technique used to image internal structures of the body, especially soft tissues (tissues other than bone).

Multiple Sclerosis (MS)—loss of patches of the protective covering (myelin sheath) of nerves, which slows the progress of nerve impulses, causing symptoms including weakness, incoordination, speech and visual disturbances. MS is typically long–term, with remissions and relapses over many years.

Post–Polio Syndrome (PPS)—a somewhat recently labeled term for new symptoms and functional loss in former polio patients who have had a long period (ten to forty years) of stability. Symptoms include weakness, fatigue, muscle or joint pain, decreased endurance, new muscle wasting, and other symptoms, which may occur in patients who were originally non–paralytic as well as paralytic.

Rheumatoid Arthritis (RA)—a chronic disease characterized by pain, stiffness, limitation of motion, and inflammation of the joints. Marked deformity of the joints can be seen in late stages. Inflammation of the arteries, nerves, eye, spleen, and other organs may also occur.

Sciatic Nerve—this nerve extends bilaterally from the spinal cord down the back of the thighs to nerves in the leg and foot.

Glossary Bibliography

Dorland's Illustrated Medical Dictionary, 26th Edition, Philadelphia, 1981.
Frank H. Netter, M.D., *Atlas of Human Anatomy*, Novartis, East Hanover, NJ, 1997.

Internet References

http://health.yahoo.com/health/Diseases_and_Conditions/Disease_
    Feed_Data/Attention_Deficit_Disorder_ADD_/(accessed 9/21/00)
http://www.graylab.ac.uk/cgi–bin/omd??Magnetic+Resonance+
    Imaging (accessed 9/21/00)
http://www.ott.zynet.co.uk/polio/lincolnshire/index1.html#whatpps
    (accessed 8/31/00)
http://www.rehabnet.com/monographs/autodys.htm (accessed 8/31/00)

ISBN 1425114989

Made in the USA
Lexington, KY
04 January 2010